printmaking
+ MIXED MEDIA

simple techniques and projects for paper and fabric

DORIT ELISHA

INTERWEAVE.
interweavestore.com

Editor Darlene D'Agostino
Art Director/Designer Karla Baker
Photographers Ann Swanson and Joe Coca
Technical Editors Jane Dunnewold and Ann Swanson
Production Katherine Jackson

Interweave Press LLC
201 East Fourth Street
Loveland, CO 80537-5655 USA
interweavestore.com

Printed in China by Asia Pacific Offset.

Library of Congress Cataloging-in-Publication Data

Elisha, Dorit.
 Printmaking + mixed media : simple techniques and projects for paper
and fabric / Dorit Elisha.
     p. cm.
 Includes bibliographical references and index.
 ISBN 978-1-59668-095-1 (pbk. : alk. paper)
1. Prints--Technique. 2. Handicraft. I. Title. II. Title:
Printmaking and mixed media. III. Title: Simple techniques and projects
for paper and fabric.
 NE860.E45 2009
 760.28--dc22

                                        2008054392

10 9 8 7 6 5 4 3 2 1

{ dedication }

To my mother, who empowered me to become the person and artist that I am.

TABLE OF CONTENTS

ORIGINAL

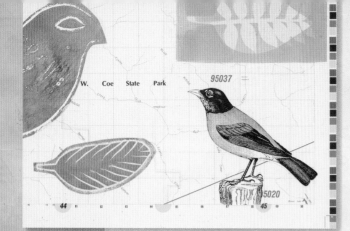

W. Coe State Park
95037

44   45   95020

95140

BIRDS SEEM TO

SAY

25   95032

Lexington
Reservoir
Recreation
Area

95030

Redwood
Estates

20   21

95135

SAN JOSE

95139

95037   35

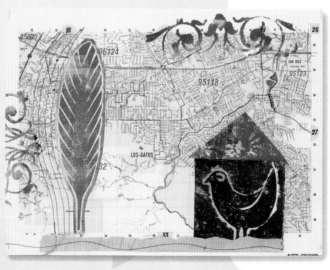

95030   18   26

95124   SAN JOSE
95123
95118

LOS GATOS

SARATOGA

MONTE SERENO

95070

24

95032

PRINTMAKING: an introduction

I discovered printmaking almost 20 years ago, while taking graphic design classes at a local community college. While being introduced to several techniques, the part I enjoyed most was when the teacher gave us the freedom to print on "found papers." Found papers were anything I could find, not the specialized (and expensive!) fine art papers normally used by printmakers.

At the time I happened to have some small Japanese papers, and I decided to collage them onto larger textured papers. This collage then became my printing surface onto which I screen printed different Asian motifs and some vintage portraits of women. To add texture to the mix, I machine-stitched over the collaged print and added some lace and bits of fabric.

I was hooked. And so began my love of mixed-media printmaking. I have been mixing papers, fibers, and printing techniques ever since.

Most fine-art students and artists mainly use specialized, expensive papers to print on, and often they will use a press to create a print. They will treat the finished print as a precious, fragile work of art, will handle the print with gloved hands, and will store it in a protective drawer.

My approach is quite different. My printmaking does not require fine-art paper. In fact, I encourage printing on any type of paper available to you, from maps and sheet music to junk mail and recycled manila folders. This saves time and money, encourages creative experimentation, and minimizes the landfill.

My printmaking is easy, and the techniques I employ do not require a press nor toxic chemicals. With just a small investment in a few tools, inks, and paints, you can begin printmaking right away! Take a peek at the chapters in this book and you will see that many prints can be made with materials you probably already own.

But perhaps most importantly, when my print is "finished," rather than treating it as a completed piece of art, I alter it and integrate it into new pieces of art, such as collage, artist books, three-dimensional pieces, and fiber art. I cut it, tear it, glue it, stitch it, or paint over it. I may even print over it again or use it as a background for another work of art.

Printmaking is addicting and fun, and this book shares these wonderful, easy, and safe techniques while showing several ways to use the finished prints in mixed-media art. Of course, it will be tempting to hang on to your finished prints as works of art in their own right, and many would probably deserve such treatment, but I hope this book will inspire you to further explore the different sides of printmaking and the many possibilities of creating mixed-media art with prints. Soon you will discover that printmaking is a fantastic way to add content, color, texture, and interest to your creations, and even the less than perfect prints can be used as components in your final mixed-media art!

Dorit Elisha

42924

chapter one

A Primer for **Printmaking**

UNDERSTANDING PRINTMAKING
BASICS WILL ENSURE SUCCESSFUL RESULTS

Printmaking is an art form that appeals to artists of all skill levels. It can be very simple, so much so that a child or an emerging artist can create prints with great success. But it also can challenge the seasoned artist who wishes to create rich and complicated artwork with multiple layers. Perhaps the best part of printmaking is the process—even before you achieve the final print, the journey there is very satisfying. There is an element of discovery, mystery, and surprise, as well as a great reward at the end of the process,

no matter which printmaking technique you are working with. Once you add other artistic media to the mix, it becomes an endless celebration of creative possibilities!

To help you begin your printmaking journey, this chapter will introduce you to the basic terms of printmaking. It also will answer basic printmaking questions and educate you on the necessary tools and the variety of surfaces on which you can print. Of course, your introduction to printmaking would not be complete without tips for success.

What Is Printmaking?

Printmaking is the process of transferring an image from a matrix to a substrate with the possibility of identical repetition (called editions). This means that once you create your design or image you can print it (several times in most cases) onto paper, fabric, wood, etc., using ink and a few additional tools. The number of different looks you can achieve using the different techniques and materials is infinite, and all you need to start is an idea, some paper, and ink.

Printmaking has been around since the invention of paper in China, almost 2,000 years ago. At its inception, it was a means of communication as it allowed for the mass production and dissemination of social, political, and historical ideas. Today, it is widely used as an artistic process.

There are enough printmaking techniques in this book to keep you busy throughout the year. Many of these techniques were used to create this colorful calendar. The backgrounds were screen printed and layered with additional cut-out prints that were attached with glue and stitching.

Screen, collagraph, sun, gelatin monotype, and relief prints on paper with stitching

6" W × 12" H (15.24 × 30.48 cm)

The botanical designs on these calendar pages are an example of gelatin monotype printing (pages 64–65).

These two images are examples of collagraph printing (pages 68–69). In collagraph printing, you create a collage to use as a printing plate.

Printing Methods

There are four basic approaches to creating the printing surface. Two of the approaches, relief and stenciling, will be discussed at length in this book. The other two approaches, intaglio and lithography, are more advanced and require more sophisticated tools and supplies.

RELIEF PRINTING involves removing most of the print block surface, leaving the raised parts of the block to be inked and printed. Examples of this method are the wood-block and linoleum-cut techniques.

The INTAGLIO method reverses the carving process. The lines of the design are incised into a printing block. After the block is inked, it is gently wiped, leaving ink only in the grooves and incisions. These inked lines will create the image on the print. An example of this method is etching.

LITHOGRAPHY is a printing method in which the surface, usually a stone or specially prepared metal plate, is not actually carved. Instead, a grease crayon is used to create an image on the plate. The surface is dampened and then it is inked. The damp areas resist the ink, so only the greasy area prints.

STENCILING is a process by which ink is forced onto the substrate (paper, fabric, etc.) through a shaped template. Screen printing is an example of sophisticated stenciling, because the paint is applied through the screen and through the open stencil surface.

Even images as delicate as a *papel picado*, a hand-cut banner made of tissue paper used during Day of the Dead festivities, can be turned into a print. With the help of a thermal-imaging printer, this image from such a banner was burned onto a screen and then screen printed onto paper.

"Untitled"

Thermal screen print on painted paper

8½" W × 11" H (21.59 × 27.94 cm)

The print shown left is an example of a mono-type print. Blue ink was applied to a plate in a painterly fashion. Then, orange ink was applied to the same plate to resemble flowers and the print was pulled. Once the print was dry, cut-outs of collagraph prints were then adhered on top.

"Spring Flowers"

Collagraph print on monoprint background with watercolor pencils

12" W × 14" H (30.48 × 35.56 cm)

For this monotype print, a photograph was laid under a glass plate and used as a guide. The image was traced using watercolor paints and a brush and then the print was pulled.

"Riding His Horse"

Monotype print with watercolor on printmaking paper

12" W × 14" H (30.48 × 35.56 cm)

BASIC PRINTMAKING VOCABULARY

Printmaking is a varied art form. Once an interest is cultivated, there's no doubt that you will develop a heightened awareness to printmaking in all forms. The definitions below will help expand your understanding of common terms in the field.

BLOCK PRINT A print made from a carved block of wood, linoleum, styrofoam, etc.

COLLAGRAPH A print made from a dimensional collaged plate.

COPYRIGHT The rights owned by an artist on an image or artwork; artwork cannot be used without the express permission of the artist who created the original work.

EDITION A complete series of identical prints pulled from a single plate (it is common for an artist to sign and number each impression within an edition).

GHOST PRINT A print pulled from the remaining image left on a plate after the first print has been pulled.

IMPRESSION A single image printed on paper, cloth, or another substrate.

LIMITED EDITION An edition with a set number of prints; limited editions increase the value of a print because of limited availability.

MASKING Covering a section of the substrate, the image, or the matrix to prevent contact with ink; masking protects the printing that already exists, so additional printing can be added without covering up the first layer.

MATRIX The source of a print—the surface on which a printable image exists.

MONOPRINT A unique print that is pulled from a ghost plate that has had an additional ink added to it or that was otherwise modified.

MONOTYPE PRINT A unique print that cannot be duplicated.

ORIGINAL PRINT A first-edition print as opposed to a reproduction.

PLATE The matrix, or surface, for certain printmaking techniques, such as monotype print or collagraph; it can be made of glass, acrylic glass, or other nonporous materials (for monotype prints), or from cardboard, fabric, and textured materials (for collagraph prints).

PRINT An impression that is the result of transferring an image from a matrix onto a substrate.

PRINTING PRESS A mechanical device that creates a print by applying pressure to the layers: the inked matrix (such as an inked collagraph plate) and a substrate (such as paper).

PROOF A print or prints retained by the artist for personal use; these are normally created prior to the printing of an edition and allow the artist to critique and improve the matrix prior to printing.

TO PULL A PRINT The act of transferring an image from a matrix to a substrate.

REGISTRATION A system used when more than one color or more than one image is aligned onto the same substrate; registration secures the exact placement of each component on the substrate.

REPRODUCTION A print produced mechanically from an existing impression—a copy of an original print.

SILKSCREEN A polyester mesh (historically, screens were made of silk) stretched over a wooden or aluminum frame on which a design can be applied using any number of different applications; the benefit of a silkscreen is the stabilization of the printing surface, which allows a clean print—one that can be duplicated many times.

SCREEN PRINT A print made by forcing ink through the screen mesh using a squeegee.

SUBSTRATE The printed surface, such as fabric, paper, metal, stone, wood, and parchment.

SUN PRINT Also known as a blue or cyanotype print, this print is made by a solar reaction to light-sensitive material applied to fabric or paper that has been partially masked by an object.

THERMOFAX PRINT A print made from a screen or mesh that had an image burned onto it by a Thermofax machine (also known as a thermal-imaging printer); also known as a thermal print.

VIGNETTE A fragment within a composition or illustration.

Printmaking Tools

If you wish to incorporate printmaking into your library of mixed-media techniques, you'll certainly want to investigate some new tools. The tools listed below are common to the printmaking techniques explained in this book and would be helpful additions to your cache of art supplies. In this book, your own hand is one of the most important burnishing tools for creating a monotype print or a collagraph print; however, there are other tools listed below that will yield a very similar effect.

ACRYLIC GLASS SHEETS Use them (⅛" to ¼" thick) as a plate for mixing or softening ink, to spread ink with a brayer, and as a matrix for monotype prints and monoprints. Picture-frame glass or a transparency sheet can also be used.

BAREN This handheld disk is used to burnish a print, typically relief prints. A well-made baren allows a printmaker to apply even pressure when transferring the ink to the printing paper. It is recommended for printing with water-based ink from a wooden block.

BONE FOLDER A bone folder is a small handheld tool used for scoring, folding, creasing, smoothing, and burnishing paper.

BRAYER Use this hand roller to transfer ink from a mixing plate and to spread it onto the printing plate. For printmaking purposes, rubber brayers in a variety of sizes are recommended.

CARBON PAPER In screen and relief printing, this paper is one of the ways to transfer patterns and images onto screens or relief-printing blocks.

CARVING TOOLS These cutting tools feature blades that are curved or angled and are used to carve designs into relief-printing blocks.

DRAWING FLUID This solution is used in screen printing in conjunction with screen filler to create a positive image on a screen. Use the drawing fluid to create a design on the screen, fill the remainder of the screen with screen filler, wash away the drawing fluid, and print your image.

FRAME In screen printing, it is the structure that supports the fabric screen and the stencil applied to the screen. The "inside" of the frame is the recessed side where the ink is deposited and pulled to create the design; the "outside" of the frame is the flat side to which the stencil is attached (see images on page 17). You can purchase screened frames or, for the techniques described in this book, create your own from stretcher frames, old picture frames, embroidery frames, and mesh.

GELATIN It is a gelling agent that can be used to create monotype prints and monoprints. Once the gelatin is mixed and has set, it can be used as an ink plate to create prints.

GLASS SHEETS During the photo-emulsion screen-printing process and sun printing, glass sheets are used as weights to secure developing images.

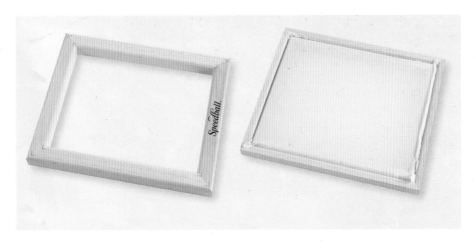

When screen printing, you attach the stencil to the outside of the frame (left) and deposit the ink to the inside of the frame (far left).

LINOLEUM BLOCK A linoleum block is hard wood with a plate of linoleum adhered to one side. The surface is very hard and cannot be cut without using linoleum cutters and/or a very sharp knife. They are used for relief prints. As an alternative, soft carving blocks made of a more rubbery material are used in this book.

SCREEN FILLER A water-based resist, filler is applied to the screen mesh to generate an impermeable background. Prior to the application of the filler, a design is drawn onto the screen surface using a chemical that dissolves when subjected to water (screen drawing fluid). Used in tandem, filler is coated onto the screen after the drawing fluid dries. Both chemicals must dry completely. Water is then sprayed onto the screen mesh and the drawing fluid dissolves, opening up the part of the screen surface that will eventually print. The filler is water resistant and becomes the background on the screen.

SOFT PENCIL A drawing tool with soft, oily, fragile graphite that, when pressure is applied, will leave a dark mark. It is useful during relief printing for transferring an image onto a printing block or for sketching a design directly onto the printing block.

SQUEEGEE A tool with a flat, smooth, rubber blade used in screen printing for pushing ink through the mesh frame. To ensure full coverage, the squeegee should be ½" to 1" (1.3 to 2.5 cm) larger on both sides than the image to be printed and 1" (2.5 cm) smaller than the inside of the frame.

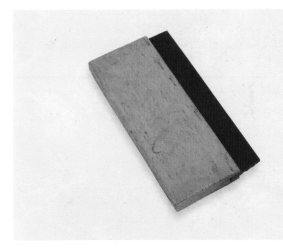

A squeegee is necessary for screen printing. For thermal printing, squeegees are typically too large for the delicate frames; it is recommended to use a smaller piece of hard plastic, an old credit card, or a ruler to pull the ink through the screen.

SKETCHING TOOLS Objects that you may use to sketch designs, both on paper, screens, and directly onto an inked plate. When monotype printing, it's a good idea to have several on hand, such as skewers and paintbrush tips in varying widths.

STENCIL Stencils are templates used in screen printing; they are the physical negative of the printed image. The stencil masks the screen so that ink is pushed only through the open space, thereby creating the printed design. They can be purchased or made from a variety of materials, such as paper and transparency sheets.

STENCIL REMOVER Liquid cleaner for removing screen filler from the screen during screen printing. Available at art-supply stores or online, it will make cleaning screens much easier than using bleach.

TRANSPARENCY SHEETS Clear, acetate film that can be used in a variety of ways for a variety of techniques. For example, transparencies printed with a design on a photocopier or computer printer can be used for sun printing and as a screen positive for exposing a screen coated with photo emulsion. If you plan to use the sheets in a computer printer, note that sheets are available for either inkjet or laser printers; using the wrong transparency could damage your printer.

Printmaking Colorants

An array of printmaking inks exist to suit your needs. Listed below are those recommended for the techniques in this book. These are water-based printing inks. They are nontoxic, easy to clean, and print beautifully on a variety of surfaces.

Keep inks stored in their containers and close them as soon as you are finished using them. Scrape excess ink from your screen and return it to its container. If the ink was from a tube, transfer excess to another container with a tight-fitting lid. In warm weather, water-based inks may grow mold. Simply scrape off the mold and use the rest of the ink as is.

ACRYLIC PAINT This highly versatile colorant can be mixed to resemble watercolor, and it can be mixed with other acrylic-based mediums for unique effects. It is water-resistant when dry and has a fast drying time for those who prefer to work quickly. Some printing techniques such as gelatin monotype and monotype printing can be accomplished with these inexpensive paints.

BLOCK-PRINTING INK Water-based and easy to clean, they have a matte finish. Formulated for relief printing, they work well with other techniques.

Block-printing ink is recommended for collagraph, gelatin monotype, and relief printing. It has a thicker consistency than screen-printing ink.

MONOTYPE INKS These highly pigmented archival inks have a thin consistency, which require some experimentation for best results, but the benefit is gorgeously saturated, permanent color. They are available in a variety of consistencies.

SCREEN-PRINTING INK Screen-print inks may be formulated specifically for textiles or paper. Some paints are metallic, an indication that mica or other light reflecting components have been added to the recipe. All are water soluble, meaning they clean up with water when wet but are permanent when dry.

WATERCOLOR PAINTS For monotype prints that call for soft color, try printing with watercolor. Experiment with using a wet plate to print on dry paper or try a dry plate on soaked paper. Tubed watercolor paints are recommended over pan watercolors. Please note that when using watercolor prints in mixed-media projects, they can bleed if wet.

Screen-printing inks are formulated for paper and for fabric. For the purposes of this book, either can be used. Fabric inks are only mandatory if you are printing on fabric that will be washed.

Monoprint ink and acrylic paint should be used for monotype prints. They both are optimal for achieving painterly effects. Acrylic paint is less expensive, but the resulting prints will not be as sharp. Acrylic is recommended for gelatin monotype prints.

Before You Begin

There are tricks and tips that make studio set-up easier for print-making. Consider these as you plan your printmaking explorations.

Setting Up the Workspace

Printmaking requires a certain amount of space. You'll need to designate a working area and a drying area. Protect the work surface from inks and spills by covering it with a reusable drop cloth. Also protect floors and other surfaces in the drying area from potential drips, and protect yourself with gloves and a smock. If possible, plan printmaking sessions in a room with running water and keep a stack of old towels handy for cleanup. Printmaking is messy, but you can minimize the mess by closing inks securely when finished. When you are cleaning up, be careful not to clog your drain—avoid disposing of inks anywhere else but in the trash.

Safety First

Although the printmaking materials in this book are nontoxic, caution must be taken during printmaking. As you progress as a printmaker, you may find yourself experimenting with materials that could be hazardous.

Create your prints in a well-ventilated area. Be sure to protect your skin and eyes from printing materials, especially if you are working with chemical substances. Avoid eating and drinking in the workspace as inadvertent ingestion of harmful substances can happen. Always wash your hands when finished printing. Label everything clearly. If you *must* work with solvents, whether cleaning agents or other chemicals, pour the solvent on a rag first and then clean the plate or screen, and always wear gloves to protect your hands from the chemicals. Immediately dispose of saturated rags to keep the air clean. It is *very* important to dispose of rags that have been subjected to solvents, rather than allowing them to stack up in the studio. Fires can instantaneously combust from the heat that builds up in a pile of rags laced with turpentine or other flammable chemicals. Keep children away from anything that is not water-based. This includes using solvents in an environment where fumes may disperse through a duct system into other parts of the house. Just because children or pets are in other rooms does not keep them safe from the chemicals you may use for printmaking. Always err on the side of caution.

Keep sharp tools up and away from children as well. If you work with stacks of paper, it's easy for cutting tools to hide among the sheets. Be mindful of this. Put away tools when finished or stab the sharp ends of knives into an old eraser. It's always a good idea to have masks, gloves (dust inside of gloves with baby powder to ease perspiration), and first-aid kits handy.

Tips for Good Printmaking

There are a few general rules to remember when printmaking. Following this advice will ensure a printmaking session that is enjoyable and productive. As you get started, remember, trial and error is the cornerstone of printmaking. Don't be discouraged if you are not 100 percent successful with the first print you create. It takes some practice to master these techniques. But it's worth the effort to become proficient.

THE REVERSE IMAGE

Keep in mind that when you are printing using some of the techniques described in this book, the printed image will be the reverse of the image on the screen, monotype plate, collagraph plate, or the relief block. To help avoid this common mistake during the first few times you print, go through the motions of the whole process without really using the ink. Pay attention to the step where you flip the plate or the block and just visualize your image printed. If it feels right, then go ahead and print.

HAVE A FINE-TIP BRUSH HANDY

No matter what technique you are working with, some imperfections happen. If you are looking for a perfect print where the ink covers the entire designated area, use a brush with a bit of ink on it to touch up small, "imperfect" spots. Colored pencils can be used to fill in blank spots as well.

ALWAYS PRINT EXTRAS

To be on the safe side and to have exactly what you need when you start your mixed-media artwork, it is a good idea to print extras. If you don't use them on the specific project they were intended for, you will find other opportunities to use them, such as in your journal or a small greeting card.

THE RIGHT PAPER, THE RIGHT PRESSURE

Since the printmaking techniques presented in this book are all done by hand, the pressure provided by a burnishing tool (rather than a printing press), insures best results. Combine papers of a lighter weight with strong hand pressure while burnishing. The monoprint journal on pages 106–107 is the only exception, as it requires heavier paper.

Remember that your print will always be the reverse image of your plate. In order for the print to read correctly, the image on the plate needs to be backward.

Relief print on paper

8" W × 6" H (20.32 × 15.24 cm)

GETTING A CLEAR PRINT

Steady and even. These two words can be used to describe how to lay a substrate onto a plate, how to burnish the image from the plate to the substrate, and how to remove the substrate from the plate. Anything else will create a blurred image or an image with uneven ink deposits. Of course, a little imperfection might also enhance your designs with a signature touch. During printmaking, you will want to move with a little bit of speed, otherwise your inked plate could dry or your paper could become "glued" to the plate.

TEST PRINTS

The first few prints pulled from a plate are the test prints, or artist's proofs. Proofs allow you to evaluate the design and the technical side of your print (the ink quality, resulting color, and evenness of the pulled print). For example, if relief printing, you may decide to refine the design of a relief block with a few closer cuts. You also can experiment with ink application, color mixing, and more. Always create your proofs with scratch paper before moving on to more costly materials, such as fabric or high-quality paper.

SEALING YOUR PRINTS

Water-based media is intermixable, which makes it very versatile, but some, such as water-based inks, will run or smear if they get wet again. It's a fantastic idea to seal your prints once dry. For water-based media, use a spray fixative to seal.

Steady, even hand pressure will ensure your prints are successful.

Storing Your Prints

As you begin to include prints in your mixed-media art, you will discover that this type of art making is a process and the act of making the print is simply one step. As such, you may find it most efficient to schedule printmaking sessions, during which you focus solely on printmaking. You will quickly begin to amass prints. Therefore, you should think about storing your prints.

STORAGE IDEAS

Prints are best stored flat, away from sunlight and dust. The least expensive way to store prints would be inside sturdy envelopes. Slip sheets of acid-free glassine paper should be placed between the sheets (acid-free paper won't cause chemical reactions with your prints, leaving them to yellow and become brittle). Label the envelopes and store on open shelves. Portfolios with dust-proof flaps are also an option.

Those who enjoy a good yard sale and wish to really protect their prints should look for metal blueprint file cabinets; tool cabinets with wide, narrow drawers; discarded paper racks; or modular shelving units—all excellent ways to store prints.

The botanical and bird prints on this collage were created over the course of several printmaking sessions. Printing several copies of the prints made for a beautiful and dynamic piece.

"Floral Landscape"

Collagraph, screen, and gelatin monotype prints on wallpaper with stitching

16" W × 22" H (40.64 × 55.88 cm)

Choosing a Printing Surface

The surface on which you print is called the substrate. Depending on the printing technique that you choose, practically anything can be a substrate. The most popular substrate is paper, which is available in a vast array of styles and types. Purchasing paper for printing is one option, but first look around your home for other possibilities. The texture, color, and thickness of your substrate will affect the printing result. Choose several substrates and print the same design on each one. Then, when you are ready to use your prints in a mixed-media creation, you will have a selection of exciting options.

Search your mixed-media treasure chest to find interesting printing surfaces. These four solid and painted papers and maps made great backgrounds for printing.

TRY PRINTING ON . . .
The following list scratches the surface when it comes to suitable printing substrates.

white paper • colored paper • painted paper • collaged paper • junk mail • newspaper • butcher paper • cardboard • paper bags • wallpaper • watercolor paper • book pages • atlas and map paper • sheet music • canvas • leather • bark • wood surfaces • white fabric • dyed fabric • printed fabric • stitched fabric • vintage fabrics

"287012 (fruit fly)"

Relief print on cotton

10" W × 10" H (25.4 × 25.4 cm)

Elin Waterston

The fruit fly and polar bear images on these art quilts are the result of relief printing on fabric with acrylic paint.

"42924 (polar bear)"

Relief print on cotton

10" × 10" (25.4 × 25.4 cm)

Elin Waterston

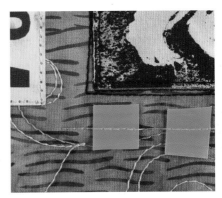

25

chapter two

Screen **Printing**

USE THIS EASY TECHNIQUE TO CREATE PRINTS BOTH PHOTOGRAPHIC AND PAINTERLY IN EFFECT

Screen prints conjure images of large, bold, multi-colored artworks featuring high-contrast photographic images. But please don't pigeon-hole the screen print to modern, pop art images. Screen printing has a softer side as well, and it includes a variety of applications. In this chapter, four screen-printing techniques are explored: screen printing with a paper stencil, screen printing with drawing fluid and screen filler, the photo-graphic emulsion process, and the thermal imaging process. All are used to create a stencil that is attached to or burned on the screen. The stencil blocks out the negative image, leaving the positive image open to allow ink to pass through and create the print. The effects can be modern and photographic or painterly. They will no doubt add a new dimension to your mixed-media creations.

What Is Screen Printing?

A screen print is created when ink is pushed through a screened frame that has been partially masked. The masked design is the negative image of the printed design. Using a squeegee, the printmaker pushes the ink through the unmasked space on the screen and onto the substrate. It is the method of choice for artists who wish to most easily create bold prints in multiple colors. You can screen print on paper, fabric, wood, as well as some unusual flat surfaces, such as large leaves. In the portrait below, the image of the woman's face was screen printed with the thermal-imaging screen-printing process on pages 52–53. The color of the papers on which the face was printed create the skin tone and hair highlights.

Screen printing is an excellent technique to use when you wish to print a photographic image. The result is often a very modern, high-contrast image absent of fine detail.

"Pride"

Thermal and collagraph prints on paper

12"W × 12" H (30.48 × 30.48 cm)

This piece is a shrine to Neta, a young girl who passed away at the age of eighteen. Her name means "sapling," a young tree. The print was created from a photograph taken by her family.

"The Sapling (Neta)"

Found wooden frame, metal branch and leaves, acrylic paint, screen print

15" W × 20" H (38.1 × 50.8 cm)

Basic Tips

With practice, screen printing is easy to master. It is a process that re-quires attention to detail. As you print, take note to how much ink you use, how your stencil is attached to your screen, and how you hold the squeegee. Make adjustments as you go to improve upon your printing.

Tools

Screen printing requires just a few tools, and they could be made by hand or purchased. For screen printing, you should have the following materials on hand: frame with mesh (preferably hinged to a wooden board), squeegee, substrate to print on (paper, fabric, etc.), screen-printing ink, your choice of material to mask the screen, and plastic spoons or knives for each color of ink you use.

Immediately clean the ink from the screen af-ter printing as dried ink will ruin a screen. Remove excess ink with a piece of cardboard and return it to the jar for reuse. In most cases, washing a screen with warm water and a soft scrubbing tool will be enough to clean it. Stencil remover is available to get rid of tougher substances, such as screen filler. Check the label of any solvent-based cleaners you use and be sure to protect your skin and eyes from it and use it in a well-ventilated area. If you seal a print by squeegee-ing a coat of acrylic gloss through the screen and onto the print, clean the screen immediately with soap and warm water.

Keep your squeegee clean between prints and between uses. Trying to remove dried ink can lead to nicks and cuts on the blade. It is recommended to store squeegees with the blade facing up to avoid inadver-tent damage to the blade.

Preparing the Screen

Before you begin, use duct or masking tape to seal all of the edges where the mesh and the frame meet to preserve the wooden frame from long water exposure and to prevent the ink from leaking through. When ready to print, stir up the ink for even consistency and use a tongue depressor or a plastic spoon to place some ink on the top part inside your frame. When screen printing on paper, it is a good idea to avoid complete contact between the screen and the paper you print on. You should leave about ⅛" between them, so they will be in contact only when the squeegee is pulled on the screen. There should be a bit of a spring movement right after you print. If the screen and paper are in full contact the entire time, the wet ink will slip through into unwanted areas and the image will be smeared. To create this minute distance, use masking tape to attach a scrap of mat board to the outside top and bottom edges of the screen frame. This will keep the screen stable but not in direct contact.

Pulling the Print

When printing, hold the squeegee at a 45-degree angle to the surface and pull it toward you. The ink pushed through the frame will create your image on the sub-strate. Raise your frame slowly to reveal the print and let the print dry. If you wish to print an additional im-age, you will need to immediately flood the screen with ink to prevent ink from drying in the screen and dam-aging it. It will also ensure an even ink deposit on your next print by preventing dried ink from masking areas of the screen. Return the ink to the top of the frame by holding the squeegee again at a 45-degree angle and pulling it back toward the top. Only apply enough pressure to move the ink from the bottom of the frame to the top; do not apply pressure as if you were creat-ing a print and pushing it through the mesh. This will prevent the ink from drying on the screen. If you plan on a long printing session, you can add a retardant to the ink to prolong its drying time.

Basic Screen Printing
With a Paper Stencil

What follows is a tutorial on basic screen printing with a paper stencil. These screen-printing instructions are universal for the rest of the screen-printing techniques and will be referenced often.

Using a paper stencil to create a screen print is perhaps the most accessible method for beginners. It requires the fewest materials and the options are only limited to what you can draw or trace and then cut out from paper to create the stencil. You can start experimenting with regular printer paper, or you can use newsprint or contact paper. The paper stencil will adhere to the screen after the first run of ink due to the moisture in the ink, but you also should tape it to the frame.

Old family portraits are perfect subjects for mixed-media art. The tree image on the left was screen printed with a paper stencil. Heritage photographs were printed using the photo-emulsion technique on pages 48–49. The prints were then used in a collage that includes fabric and paper scraps. Stitched details and highlights with colored pencils accent the piece and add a sense of continuity.

"Childhood Memories"

Paper stencil and photo-emulsion screen prints on paper with stitching and fabric and paper scraps

12" W × 16" H (15.24 × 40.64 cm)

TECHNIQUE

1 To create the stencil, first trim a sheet of paper so that it is ½" smaller on all sides than the frame. Draw your design on the paper and cut it out using a craft knife.

2 Using the sheet with the positive image cut out, adhere the stencil to the outside of the frame with masking tape. To prevent unwanted ink spots, make sure that no mesh is exposed between the frame and the paper stencil.

3 Choose a piece of paper to print on and lay the frame on top of it, open side up (the paper stencil should be in contact with your substrate paper).

4 Apply ink all along the top part of the inside of the frame with a plastic knife. Place the squeegee between the ink and the top of the frame. Pull the squeegee at a 45-degree angle from the top of the frame and toward you while applying pressure to push the ink through the mesh.

materials

Newsprint paper, freezer paper, or contact paper for the stencil • Pencil • Scissors or craft knife • Masking tape • Screen-printing frame • Screen-printing ink • Squeegee • Substrate to print on

5 Lift the frame to check your proof print. If you are satisfied, proceed and repeat this process as many times as you like. When you are finished, remove the paper stencil and rinse the frame thoroughly.

Easy Ways to Add Color

It is easy to create a multicolored print even with just a single screen-printing stencil. It's just a matter of how you deposit the ink onto the screen. Incorporate these simple techniques into your printing for results with a lot of flair.

RAINBOW

If you desire swatches of color side by side or a gradient color effect, experiment with rainbow rolling.

TECHNIQUE

1 If using a stencil, tape the stencil to the outside of the screen (for this example, no stencil was used). Lay the screen face down onto the paper you wish to print on. Place two or three dollops of ink next to each other at the top of the open side of the screen.

2 Place your squeegee behind the ink and move it slightly left and right until the colors mix in the neighboring areas while keeping the original shade on the far sides. Push the ink through the screen with the squeegee.

3 Remove the screen and check the print. Make any desired adjustments and continue printing.

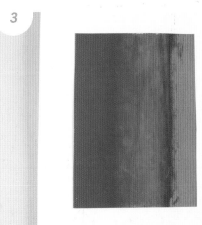

SPOT COLOR

You also can add spot color to your prints very easily.

TECHNIQUE

1

2

1 Tape the stencil to the outside of the screen. Lay the screen face down onto the paper you wish to print on. Determine where you would like the spot color to appear and dot ink onto the open side of the screen accordingly. Apply additional ink along the top of the screen. Push the ink through the screen with a squeegee.

2 Remove the screen and check the print.

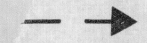

Multiscreen
Printing

Experimenting with color is one of the most fun aspects of printmaking. As you advance as a printmaker, your need for exciting color options will grow. When your prints call for a variety of color, try printing color by using a separate screen for each one. You can achieve a variety of results with this technique. For example, you can create secondary colors by layering primary colors (warning: layering all three primary colors on top of each other will create a muddy brown). If you choose this layering technique, you may want to add a transparent base to your inks. A transparent base will make the ink more transparent, act as a retardant, and add volume to the consistency. You also can introduce the color of the background paper into your palette by deliberately leaving it void of ink.

As you begin experimenting with this method, keep it simple. Start with two or three colors. It also may be helpful to color in a sketch of your design with colored pencils, which will serve as a guide. On the guide you can designate each color with a number and then create a different plate for each number. As you print, you will want to use register guides to ensure the printed layers line up in the exact same position

for each respective color. This could be as simple as an "x" marked on your work surface with some masking tape in one corner that you will keep referring to with each print. Or, it could be a more complicated system where you hinge your screen to a wooden base, tape two registration pins on one side of it and hole punch all your papers so they "match" these pins when placed under the screen. It is important to let each layer dry before moving on to the next color. The steps on the right illustrate basic multiscreen printing.

This print uses six colors and therefore required six separate stencils. The black paper was allowed to show through as the seventh color. Multilayered prints such as this one require a registration system to guarantee the right placement of each color.

"Clown"

Paper stencil screen print on paper

8" W × 10" H (20.32 × 25.4 cm)

TECHNIQUE

materials

Pencil • Paper • Craft knife • Squeegee • Screen-printing frame • Screen-printing ink • Substrate to print on

1 Sketch your image and determine how many colors your finished design will contain. Create a stencil for each color. In this example, three colors were used, and therefore three stencils were created. Because each color will relate only to part of the design, cut out this part and the remaining area will act as a mask.

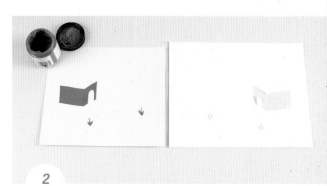

2 Print the first color according to the instructions on page 31 ("paper stencils" Steps 3, 4, and 5). Allow the print to dry completely and wash the screen.

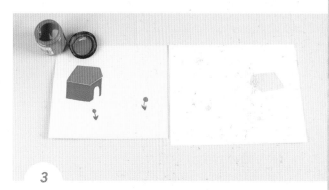

3 Use the registration mark to line up the screen and the stencil for the second color with the previous print. Print the second color. Allow the print to dry completely and wash the screen.

4 Repeat the previous step for the third color.

35

This is another example of a screen print with six colors, and therefore six stencils were used to create the individual colors. In this example, green and purple dot the composition; they are an example of the spot-color technique discussed on page 33.

"Still Life"

Paper stencil screen print on paper

10" W × 8" H (25.24 × 20.32 cm)

These pieces were inspired by architectural drawings. The geometric shapes signify a bird's eye view of a city landscape.

"Untitled"

Paper stencil screen print on watercolor paper with monoprint and drawing

10" W × 8" H (25.24 × 20.32 cm)

Dorit Elisha and Kyoko Fischer

Bottom

22" W × 15" H (55.88 × 38.1 cm)

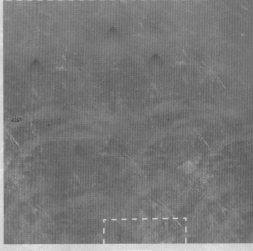

Screen Printing
With a Drawing-Fluid Resist

In this technique, you will create a resist by drawing directly on the screen with drawing fluid. Drawing fluid is painted directly on the screen to create the positive image you wish to print. It is used in conjunction with screen filler, a solution used to mask the screen. Drawing fluid is blue in color and screen filler is brown, so they are easy to see when applied to the screen. You can use most anything to apply the drawing fluid but will use a squeegee to apply the screen filler.

The screen for this print was designed with drawing fluid and screen filler. A paintbrush dipped in drawing fluid was used to trace a photograph that was laid under the screen (you can place a transparency over the photo to protect it). The printed image has a definite drawn quality only achievable with this technique.

"Untitled"

Photo-emulsion screen print on paper with collage

20" W × 8" H (50.8 × 20.32 cm)

TECHNIQUE

materials

Pencil • Paper • Drawing fluid • Screen filler • Paintbrush •
Warm water • Squeegee • Screen-printing frame • Screen-
printing ink • Substrate to print on

1 Choose an image to create the print. You can sketch the image or use a photograph or a copyright-free image.

2 Place the frame screen-side down on top of the image. Trace the drawing directly onto the inside of the screen with a pencil.

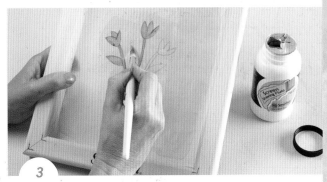

3 Shake the drawing fluid. Lift the screen from the work surface and use a paintbrush to fill in the traced image with the fluid. Lean the screen against the wall to dry completely.

4 Stir the screen filler and place the bottle in warm water for a few minutes. Using a squeegee, spread the filler all over the screen and let it dry completely.

5

6

5 Once the filler is dry, use cold water to wash off the drawing fluid (high water pressure recommended). The area to be printed will now be exposed.

6 Proceed with your printing as described on page 31 ("paper stencil" Steps 3, 4, and 5). When finished, clean your screen with stencil remover to remove the filler material.

These horses were printed using the drawing fluid and screen-filler technique onto a background that was created with the monotype-printing technique on pages 58–59. The top and bottom borders are collages that were stitched to the piece. To finish, the collages were accented with fibers.

"Prairie Horses"

Drawing fluid and screen-filler screen print on monotype background with collage, fibers, and stitching

14" W × 12" H (35.56 × 30.48 cm)

These prints and the prints on page 37 were created as a collaboration between two artists. Each started two prints and then switched. The abstract shapes on these prints were created with the drawing fluid and screen-filler screen-printing technique described on the previous pages.

"Untitled"

Drawing-fluid and screen-filler screen print on monotype background

10" W × 8" H (25.24 × 20.32 cm)

Dorit Elisha and Kyoko Fischer

Bottom

22" W × 22" H (55.88 × 55.88 cm)

THE TORTILLA CURTAIN PROJECT

When a group of printmakers gather under one vision to create art, the result is rich with the creative perspective of each artist. Printmaking is a great way to collaborate with other artists—combining prints is an easy way to unify diverse points of view and artistic styles into a cohesive piece rich with personality. The process is fun, educational, surprising, and it is a great tool for community building.

The collection of artwork that follows is an example of a collaborative printmaking project called, "The Tortilla Curtain." The project was inspired by the book of the same title by T. C. Boyle. Twenty printmakers participated in the project. These printmakers form a group that meets regularly at the Foothill Community College in Los Altos, California. Participants had different printmaking backgrounds, such as screen printing, monoprinting, letterpress, block printing as well as experience in other art media.

The project lasted two months and included several discussions regarding the controversial theme. The result was eighty mixed-media prints. At least three artists have contributed to each print. This collaboration gave the participants an opportunity to exchange ideas, learn new techniques, solve problems, and respond to other artists' voices.

As you create, consider collaborating with other artists to reap similar benefits.

A drawing of a very determined woman and an image of a Buddha sculpture are juxtaposed in this print, reflecting one of the main characters and an important object in the story. The drawing of the woman was based on a photograph while the strong sculpture image was screen printed over the open screen background. The torn paper stencil for the sun image, the screen-printed cactus texture as well as the bright yellow color all hint to the harsh condition in the location where the story takes place.

Foothill Community College Printmakers

Paper stencil, block, and thermal-screen prints, pencil

22" W × 15" H (55.88 × 38.1 cm)

ARROYO BLANCO ESTATES

This mixed-media print demonstrates very clearly how choosing the right printmaking technique can enhance an idea: The curtains were monoprinted, meaning painted with a brush on the plate and then printed. This technique is great when you want to mimic the soft feel of fabric. It comes in sharp contrast to the image of the barbed wire that was printed using the photographic-emulsion screen-print technique, in which the fine details of the wire would be the most visible. In addition, the eye holes in the skull were monoprinted using real tortillas as the plate.

Foothill Community College Printmakers

Photo-emulsion screen print and monotype print

15" W × 22" H (38.1 × 55.8 cm)

In this print, several printmaking techniques were chosen to create a mood: torn paper stencil (cactus), stenciling (houses), open (no stencil) screen print (for the background), pencil sketch (coyote eyes), letterpress printing, and stitching. The zigzag stitching emphasizes the texture of the thorny cactus and the deceptive "welcoming" atmosphere, just like the staring eyes of the coyote. The type that was chosen for the letterpress text was meant to remind the viewer of real estate advertising posters (one of the two female characters in the book is a real estate agent).

Foothill Community College Printmakers

Stencil screen print, air brushing, stitching

15" W × 22" H (38.1 × 55.8 cm)

What does an illegal immigrant woman dream about? Basic necessities: A house and some clothes to wear. Here the drawn face was screen printed using the photographic-emulsion technique. The dress is constructed of real fabric and stitched onto the paper with rickrack and is a reminder of old and simple clothing. There is also handpainting, stenciling, and embellishment of *milagros* (a Mexican religious decorative item).

Foothill Community College Printmakers

Photo-emulsion screen print, stencil, paint, collage, stitching

15" W × 22" H (38.1 × 55.8 cm)

This print juxtaposes two female characters: the all-American woman and a Mexican woman. The American woman is a pencil drawing with a watercolor wash; the Mexican woman is represented by a thermal print of a *papel picado*—a traditional Day of the Dead decorative paper cutout. This image was chosen for its ethnic context as well as the connection with death, which is an invisible protagonist in this book.

Foothill Community College Printmakers

Thermal and stencil screen prints, pencil, colored pencils

15" W × 22" H (38.1 × 55.8 cm)

On top of the open screen-printed background, the cactus was screen printed with a paper stencil in different colors. Here the cactus is the focal point of the print. Its size and placement help create the image of a hot and threatening environment. A small vignette is placed on the side with a drawing of the contrasting urban atmosphere described in the book.

Foothill Community College Printmakers

Paper-stencil screen print, pencil

15" W × 22" H (38.1 × 55.8 cm)

This image of a distant neighborhood on the edge of the canyon is created with a photo-emulsion screen print (homes and street sign), screen printed empty background, collagraph print ("for sale" sign), and collaged stereotypical figures of a man and a woman overlooking the landscape. The type again is contributing to the real estate theme.

Foothill Community College Printmakers

Collagraph and photo-emulsion screen prints, letterpress print, collage

15" W × 22" H (38.1 × 55.8 cm)

The raging fire is no doubt the dominant figure in this print. It was screen printed using a paper stencil. It was printed twice, in two different colors that are a bit off the registration, to evoke a feeling of movement. The collagraph-printed house and fence were attached prior to the printing of the fire, which required a partial masking of the house. In the background, there is a street sign that was screen printed with photographic emulsion as a reminder of the actual place where the fire spread.

Foothill Community College Printmakers

Monotype, stencil screen, and photo-emulsion screen prints, collage

15" W × 22" H (38.1 × 55.8 cm)

This print demonstrates the soft and feminine side of the other female character in the book via the dress. The dress is hand rendered on a screen-printed background. The face was drawn and then screen printed over a sewing pattern on tissue paper. The toy horse collage and the white barbed wire evoke the experiences of motherhood and the downtrodden, respectively.

Foothill Community College Printmakers

Collagraph, photo-emulsion screen, and paper-stencil screen prints, stitching

15" W × 22" H (38.1 × 55.8 cm)

The two figures screen printed with a torn paper stencil seem to be lost in this chaotic atmosphere around them: The background paper is covered with small printed symbols, torn collaged map pieces, fiber stitching as well as *milagros*. Adding to this "lost" feel is the fact that they are printed with a soft color that blends them with the background rather than a strong color that would imply confidence.

Foothill Community College Printmakers

Paper-stencil screen print, collage

15" W × 22" H (38.1 × 55.8 cm)

This print says it all with just a few images: Man and woman trying to grow roots in this deserted place, while a new life is being created at the same time, in the same place. The image of the hands is a digital print that was stitched onto the screen-printed background image.

Foothill Community College Printmakers

Paper-stencil and photo-emulsion screen prints, digital photo

15" W × 22" H (38.1 × 55.8 cm)

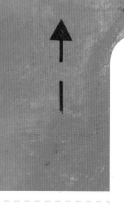

Screen Printing
With Photo Emulsion

To print a sharp image, the photo-emulsion technique is recommended. With this method, you will essentially photographically develop an image onto the screen mesh using emulsion solution and light. There are two types of emulsions—diazo and ammonium bichromate. The diazo emulsion is safer to use, but always check the manufacturer's instructions before using. It is best to use a screen made of monofilament polyester or nylon for this process. Be sure the screen is very clean (degreasing with soap and a bristle brush is recommended), otherwise, the emulsion won't adhere well to the screen and the transferred image won't be as crisp. The emulsion is light sensitive; for best results, complete this procedure in a dark room (use a red light for visibility). Cover windows with dark trash bags if necessary.

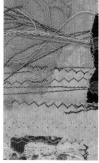

This heritage image was printed using the photo-emulsion process. Although it is the focal image, it was actually printed last. First, the background was created from leftover prints that are examples of screen and collagraph printing as well as photocopied images. These were collaged and stitched to a sheet of background paper. Once the focal image was added, colored pencils were used to enhance the design and free-form stitching was used to unify the piece.

"Vintage in Purple"

Photo-emulsion screen print on collaged background with colored pencils and free-motion stitching

16" W × 20" H (40.64 × 50.8 cm)

Using the drawing fluid, photo emulsion, or thermal screen-printing processes will allow you to work with priceless heirloom photos without altering the original.

"The Young Couple"

Photo-emulsion screen print, collage, encaustic

9" W × 6" H (22.86 x 15.24 cm)

TECHNIQUE

materials

Image photocopied onto a transparency (or hand drawn on transparency with opaque black marker) • Photo emulsion • Emulsion trough or wide ruler (recommended for small screens only) • Screen-printing frame • Dark room • Light source • A sheet of glass the size of your screen • Screen-printing ink • Squeegee • Substrate to print on • Soft bristle brush

1 Photocopy your chosen image onto a transparency sheet or create an original by using a black opaque marker and a transparency sheet. In a semi-dark room away from bright light, mix the photographic emulsion according to the manufacturer's instructions.

2 Place the screen on a protected surface on the floor and coat it with a thin, even layer of photographic-emulsion solution on both sides (use an emulsion trough or a wide ruler if working with a small screen). Apply emulsion from bottom to top in order to control the amount of solution you deposit on the screen. Let the emulsion dry in a darkened area or inside a drawer. Use a fan to speed up the process.

3 Place the frame on your work surface and the transparency on the frame with the right side facing the outside of the frame. Lay a clean piece of glass on top of the image to create a tight seal. Position a light source directly above the center of your screen to expose the image. The exposure time will be dependent on the type of solution and strength of the light source. (For more information about this technique, please visit speedballart.com.)

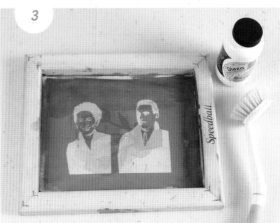

4

5

4 Use a hose to wash the screen to remove the emulsion from the image area. Wash front and back, focusing on the positive space. You can also use a soft bristle brush to clean the positive space in the image for a sharper print, but be careful not to damage the stencil. If possible, let the stencil harden overnight before printing.

5 Proceed with your printing as described on page 31 ("paper stencil" Steps 3, 4, and 5). To remove the emulsion from the screen after printing is done, wet the screen with water, spray emulsion remover on both sides of the screen, scrub for two minutes, quickly rinse with cold water and then rinse again with high pressure to make sure there are no clogged areas left.

In this book created from prints and found objects, the pages on the left show an example of portraits printed with the photo-emulsion screen-printing process. The two portraits were printed on vintage wallpaper. One was them matted with cardboard, and the other was centered in a metal frame. The book was then accented with eyelets, fibers, and found objects.

"Fairy Tales"

Photo-emulsion prints on metal frame and tile with eyelets, fibers, and found objects

7" W × 9" H × 2" D (17.78 × 22.86 × 5.08 cm)

For both of these pieces, an image of a Chinese dragon was screen printed with the photo-emulsion process on paper and hand-dyed fabric. To enhance the Asian motif, straw and Asian-inspired wall-papers were used to create mats. The pieces were further embellished with earthy fibers.

"Asian Dragon 1 and 2"

Photo-emulsion screen print on fabric with straw and patterned wallpapers and fibers

12" W × 12" H (30.48 × 30.48 cm)

Screen Printing
With a Thermal-Imaging Printer

A thermal print is a screen print created with a thermal-imaging printer (the brand name is Thermofax). Before the modern photocopier, these machines were used in schools to make copies. Today, tattoo artists use them to create copies of designs while fabric designers and artists use them to create unique prints on paper and fabric.

The thermal-imaging printer can create a screen in just a few minutes and without any chemicals. The only technical limitation is the image size—its maximum width is 8½"—but lengthwise you are limited only by the frame that will hold the screen. Thermal-imaging printers, while handy, are pricey, but used ones are available. If you don't wish to purchase a machine, you can search the Internet for companies that will burn screens for you (see page 116 for more information).

These pendants were printed with thermal screens that had different patterns burned onto them. Additional beads and findings were attached for interest and weight.

"Untitled"

Thermal prints on formica with jewelry findings

1½" W × 2½" H (3.81 × 6.35 cm)

Far Left

"Untitled"

Thermal prints on painted chipboard with metal chain, beads

1½" W × 1½" H (3.81 × 3.81 cm)

A thermal-imaging printer is quite versatile for a printmaker because it easily creates screens from just about any image. It is excellent for transferring patterns and heirloom prints that you don't wish to damage. It can also be used as an alternative to the photo-emulsion process described on pages 48–49.

TECHNIQUE

materials

Black-and-white photocopies of images • Thermal-imaging screen • Sheet of paper to create a guide • Thermal-imaging printer • Double-stick tape • Plastic screen-printing frame or custom frame created from cardboard • Screen-printing ink • Old credit card • Substrate to print on

1 Cut the screen to fit your chosen image. To prepare a guide, use a sheet of paper that is the same width as the cut screen but an inch longer. Prepare a guide by folding the top of the paper over 1" (2.5 cm).

2 Layer the guide, image, and screen. Place the guide on the bottom with the folded side up, then lay the image right side up, and top with the screen smooth side down so it is in direct contact with the image.

3 Feed the layers together, folded side up first, into the machine. As the screen runs through the machine, the image will be burned onto the screen. Remove the screen from the attached image and attach it to a plastic frame or a temporary cardboard frame with double-stick tape.

4 Proceed with your printing as described on page 31 ("paper stencil" Steps 3, 4, and 5). Note: Larger squeegees are too heavy-duty for the delicate cardboard frame. Instead, use an old credit card or a piece of hard-edged, thin plastic to push the ink across the surface.

These dolls were printed on a scrap of wallpaper. All of the printed paper pieces were stitched onto a scrap of fabric.

"Summers of Sunflowers"

Thermal prints with colored pencil on wallpaper with fabric, stitching, and collage

11" W × 11" H (27.94 × 27.94 cm)

These prints are a selection out of a series of twenty. They feature thermal-printed patterns and images (the sun and the child) printed on painted papers. To finish, additional collage images and marker-drawn details were added. They tell the visual story of relationships between men and women, adults and children, and families.

"Life Stories"

Thermal print on painted background with drawing, stamping, and collage

16" W × 20" H (40.64 × 50.8 cm)

{ chapter three }

More **Printing Techniques**

MORE PRESS-LESS TECHNIQUES TO ADD TO YOUR MIXED-MEDIA REPERTOIRE

As you dive deeper into printmaking, you'll be delighted to find that even more techniques exist that require just a few simple tools and supplies and little printmaking background. All you need to succeed is a healthy artistic appetite and craving for experimentation. In this chapter, four basic printmaking techniques are covered: monotype, collagraph, relief, and sun printing. In the professional world of printmaking, all of these techniques (save sun printing) often require a press or special equipment. Here, you'll learn how to accomplish each with the bare minimum. You'll enjoy learning that you can utilize skills you've already honed during your mixed-media adventures, such as painting and collage, to create unique and fantastic prints that will astound, whether as stand-alone works of art or incorporated into ambitious mixed-media creations.

What is Monotype Printing?

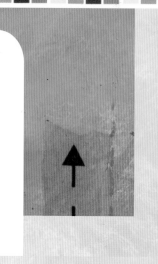

If you love painting, chances are you will love monotype printmaking. The monotype combines printmaking and painting techniques to create an impression. The word "monotype" literally means "one image." A monotype is created when an image is painted or drawn with paint or ink onto a plate and then pressed onto a substrate to create an impression. For the techniques described here, you will transfer an image to paper with your hand or a burnishing tool, instead of a press. The plate can be glass, acrylic glass, metal, or clay. When you print with the monotype technique, each successive print will be unique, unlike most other printmaking techniques that allow for the production of several identical prints. Monotypes are wonderful for creating prints with a painterly effect and abstract backgrounds for mixed-media art. When creating a design for a monotype print, your choice of drawing tool will determine the look of your piece. When applying ink to the plate or drawing on an inked plate, experiment with the ends of paintbrushes, pencil tips and erasers, sticks, a toothbrush, or your finger. You also may want to try wiping some ink away with a rag or cotton swabs. As you are introducing yourself to the medium, have fun playing with a test plate. Make marks and create designs with different inks and different drawing utensils and then pull prints to see what piques your interest and what comes naturally to you.

The artist that created this multicolored monotype print is inspired by Japanese Kanji symbols. The colors in this print were pulled one impression at a time. Ink was applied to a copper plate with a palette knife, the paper placed using guides outside the printing area, and then burnished with a potter's rib.

"Zo Ka"

Monotype print with oil-based ink on paper

9" W × 12" H (22.9 × 30.5 cm)

Midge Williams

These monotype prints started first as a collage of strips of vintage newsprint that had been painted with watercolor. Brown and black etching ink was then evenly applied to two glass plates. The collage was placed face down onto the first plate and the artist used a ballpoint pen to draw the designs onto the paper. She also lightly brushed her hand across the paper to create the distressed look. She pulled the paper, allowed it to dry, and then repeated the technique on the second plate.

"Tea Break"

Monotype print with watercolor paint on paper collage

7.5" W × 6" H (19 × 15 cm)

Birthe Lindhart

Bottom

"Coffee Break"

Monotype print with watercolor paint on paper collage

7" W × 5" H (18 × 13 cm)

Birthe Lindhart

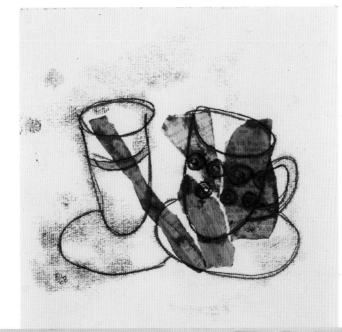

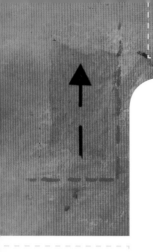

Basic
Monotype Printing

Monotypes can be created in several ways. The most traditional way is to use ink or paint to create a design on the plate and then burnish it onto paper. A variation would be to apply ink to the plate and then sketch into the ink using a sharp object, such as a skewer, pencil, or top of a paintbrush. You can also remove some of the ink with a rag to create the image. To create a line print, you could also cover an inked plate with paper, lightly draw onto the back of the paper, and then pull the print (be careful not to put any pressure on the rest of the paper to avoid staining). If creating an original design on the plate seems intimidating, place an image under a clear plate and trace it.

To create these monotype prints, the artist used monotype printing inks and a paintbrush to render the images onto a glass plate. She then covered the plate with paper, burnished them, and pulled the prints.

Top to Bottom

"The Raven," "Longing for the Full Nest," "Fall"

Monotype prints on paper

Daniela Barnea

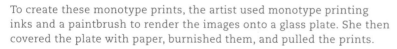

TECHNIQUE

materials

Acrylic or glass plate • Monotype ink, acrylic paint, or watercolors • Brayer • Paintbrush • Lightweight paper or watercolor paper • Burnishing tool

1 Use a paintbrush and ink to paint directly onto a piece of acrylic glass or glass plate.

2 Place a damp sheet of paper over the plate and burnish the image using the "pillow" of your hand or a baren in a circular motion. Pull the paper to reveal your print. Let it dry completely. Depending on the amount of ink left on the plate, you may be able to pull a second "ghost" print (a lighter version of the same image).

The image in this monotype print was traced from a drawing that was placed under the glass plate and used as a guide.

"Cherubs"

Monotype print on paper

10" W × 8" H (25.4 × 20.32 cm)

Monotype Printing Tips

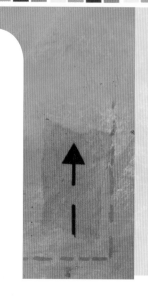

Monotype printing is as easy as painting on paper. When choosing the size of your inking plate, think about the type of border you desire. If you want an image with a full bleed, your paper should be smaller than the plate. If you desire a sharp edge around your printed image, use artist tape to mask a border and frame the area to be printed. You should experiment with different types of paper for effects. For example, Japanese paper will produce a softer effect. When using heavier paper, such as watercolor paper, mist the paper with water first and allow it to soak for a few minutes prior to printing. This is especially true if you are printing with acrylic paint. When using dry paper, you'll have to work quickly so that the ink does not dry on the plate before the print is pulled.

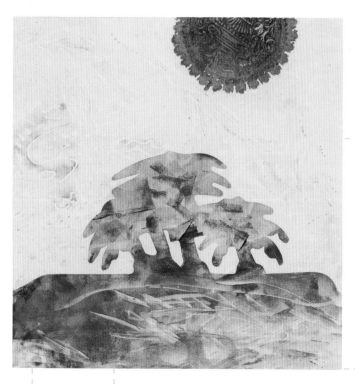

This print is a hybrid between a monotype print and a collagraph print (see pages 68–73 for more details on collagraph printing). First, a plate was cut from a piece of heavy-duty transparency. Then, the plate was painted with inks and the print pulled.

"Oasis"

Monotype and collagraph prints on paper

12" W × 12" H (30.48 × 30.48 cm)

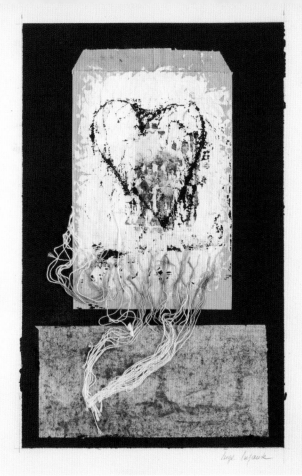

"Heartstrings"

Monotype print on paper with collage, paper bag, and fibers

14" W × 20" H (35.56 × 50.8 cm)

Inge Infante

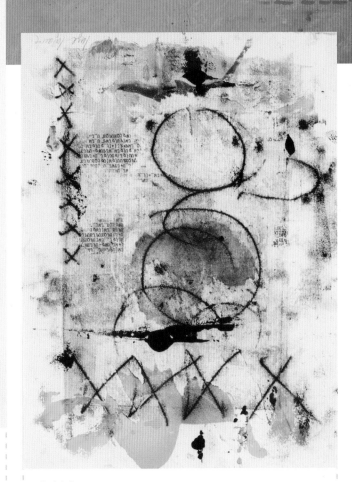

"Viola"

Monotype print on paper with collage

14" W × 20" H (35.56 × 50.8 cm)

Inge Infante

These three pieces show an interesting variation on the monotype print. Acrylic paint was spread onto a transparency sheet, and the sheet was laid on top of the collages, ink side down. The artist then used a pen and pencil to scribble on the back of the inked transparency, leaving fuzzy black lines that help unify the composition.

"PUEC"

Monotype print on paper with collage

15" W × 11" H (38.1 × 27.94 cm)

Inge Infante

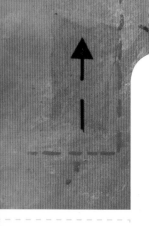

Gelatin
Monotype Printing

This is a great variation on basic monotype printing. The main difference is that instead of using a glass or acrylic glass plate you will use a gelatin plate. The plate is prepared from unflavored and color-free gelatin available at any supermarket. This technique is great when you want to print natural and textured objects, but you can also achieve a painterly type of print with it. When preparing the gelatin, use a shallow pan and follow the directions on the box, only substitute water for the juice. Before it sets, gently push aside any bubbles that appear on the surface (although, they also can make for an interesting texture). After the gelatin sets, allow it to harden in the refrigerator for about two hours. You can coat the gelatin with ink and lay flat textured objects on top and pull positive and negative images, or you can gently paint a multicolored image directly on the gelatin using paintbrushes and print it like a basic monotype.

During printing, if you wish to clean the gelatin plate from any traces of ink, lay a sheet of newspaper onto the plate, lightly burnish, and pull to remove leftover color. When finished, the gelatin can be refrigerated for up to ten days. If the surface is dented, you can place it in the microwave for a few seconds (unless the gelatin is in a metal pan) and then let it harden again. Dispose of the gelatin in your trash as it may clog drainpipes.

You can also create painterly prints with a gelatin plate. Gently paint directly on the plate and print like a monotype print.

"Still Life"

Gelatin monotype on paper

8" W × 10" H (20.32 × 25.4 cm)

In printmaking, nothing is ever trash. The leaves used to create the gelatin monotype prints on the right can be saved and used in another piece of art.

TECHNIQUE

materials

Gelatin • A shallow pan for the plate • Acrylic glass or glass plate • Brayer • Water-based block-printing ink • Acrylic paint • Textured objects (leaves, dried flowers, feathers, lace, etc.) • Variety of thin papers (regular copy paper, tissue paper, handmade paper, Asian paper, watercolor paper, etc.) cut to fit in the gelatin plate

1   Place a small amount of ink on a glass plate and coat the brayer with an even layer of ink. Use the brayer to roll the ink on the gelatin from edge to edge. If you use paint instead of ink, you can roll it directly on the gelatin because the paint doesn't need softening.

2   Choose a relatively flat textured object, such as a leaf or piece of lace—you don't want the object to dent or scratch the gelatin—and place it on the inked gelatin.

3   Place a sheet of paper on top of the gelatin and burnish the paper for ten to fifteen seconds. Be sure the entire sheet of paper makes complete contact with the ink. Pull the paper to reveal the negative image of the object. Remove the object carefully without denting the gelatin.

4

5

4 Lay a second sheet of paper onto the gelatin, burnish and pull to reveal the positive image.

5 If you wish to print a duotone image, repeat Steps 3 and 4 using a second color of ink. Use the positive print that was created with the first color to print a negative print with the second color and vice versa.

The gelatin monotype prints in this accordion book were printed on painted papers. The prints are double-sided and therefore are encased in transparent sheets so both sides can be viewed.

"A Book for Spring"

Double-sided gelatin monotype prints on painted paper with transparency sheets, ribbon, skewers, and beads

6" W × 8" H × ½" D
(15.24 × 20.32 × 1.27 cm)

Doilies make great printing surfaces—they are flat, lightweight, and their quaint detailing adds to the interest of the print. For this gelatin monotype print, botanicals were laid onto the gelatin.

"Freshly Cut"

Gelatin monotype print on fabric doily

5" W × 5" H (12.7 × 12.7 cm)

These gelatin monotype prints were printed on paper
using a variety of leaves and ink colors. When creating
gelatin prints, you can use a plate that is the same size
as your final print or you can use a smaller plate and
print in overlapping sections such as those shown here.

"Seasons Series"

Gelatin monotype prints on fabric

20" W × 22" H (50.8 × 55.88 cm)

What is Collagraph Printing?

Collagraph printing is a method of printmaking that relies on an inked dimensional but a relatively flat collage to create an image. The collage can be created with most anything textured—found papers, fabrics, lace, bubble wrap, corrugated cardboard, to name a few. Just be sure that the items chosen are all similar in dimension—the surfaces of the dimensional items need to be flush for a successful print. Collagraph prints can be created from materials you gather from around the house. Essentially to construct the plate, glue dimensional items to a sturdy surface, such as cardboard, mat board, or poster board. Once the collage dries, apply an even coat of ink and burnish onto paper.

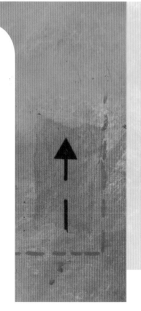

The fish on this accordion book were printed from a collagraph plate. Prior to printing, the artist sealed the collagraph plate with two coats of matte gel medium to ensure the longevity of the plate and also to make sure the images on the plate stay in place during printing.

"Where Are All the Fish . . ."

Collagraph prints on paper

6½" W × 5½" H × ¾" D (16.5 × 14 × 2 cm)

Rae Trujillo

The plate for this collagraph print was created by using a craft knife to carve figures into mat board. The additional shapes were printed from another collagraph plate—they were cut from a manila folder and glued onto a piece of cardboard. The background features a monotype print on a sheet of textured wallpaper.

"Fiesta Mexicana"

Collagraph print on painted wallpaper

16" W × 18" H (40.64 × 45.72 cm)

Elaborate designs can be formed onto a collagraph plate with the simplest of materials. This eye was constructed from a discarded file folder.

"All Knowing Eye"

Collagraph print on paper

8" W × 8" H (20.32 × 20.32 cm)

Carol Kemp

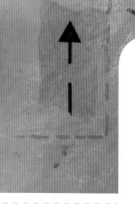

Basic
Collagraph Printing

The simplest way to create a collagraph plate is to cut shapes from a piece of sturdy paper, such as a recycled manila folder, and glue them onto a piece of cardboard. If you want to preserve your plate for future use, protect it with a few layers of matte gel medium and let it dry before you ink it the first time. Dried stains on the collagraph plate will not be transferred to the final print as long as they are not water soluble. However, you may enjoy the colored collagraph plate as a work of art in and of itself. During printing, you may need to reload ink a few times until the whole piece is evenly coated. Too much ink can cause a dark stain on your print, and not enough ink will result in a pale print. Once you print, you can use the print as is, or you can cut shapes from the print to then use in your mixed-media art.

When printing a book, take extra care to make sure the words print correctly by making a mock-up of the book first. When you produce the collagraph plate, you will need to arrange the images and words in reverse so that they will read correctly once printed.

"Buffalo Tales"

Collagraph prints on paper

2¾" W × 4¼" H × ¼" D (7 × 11.5 × .50 cm)

Rae Trujillo

TECHNIQUE

1. Create a dimensional collage (for this piece, organic shapes were cut from a recycled manila folder). Use a glue stick to adhere the items (note: wet glue can cause the paper to curl). Once all of the items are adhered, turn the collage face down on a clean flat surface and place a heavy book on top to help the collage dry flat.

2. Apply ink to an acrylic or glass plate. Roll a brayer over the ink to evenly coat it and then roll the brayer over the collaged plate. Be sure to cover the entire collage with an even layer of ink to avoid blank areas or globs of ink.

3. Place a sheet of paper on top of the inked collage and burnish with the pillow of your hand. Pull the print off and let it dry.

materials

Cardboard or similar sturdy surface to create the collagraph plate • Cardstock • Textured paper, wallpaper, or fabric • Water-based block-printing ink • Scissors • Glue stick • Acrylic or glass plate to spread the ink onto • Brayer • Thin paper to print on (white and colored)

When printing collagraphs, the collagraph plate also can be a work of art. On this plate, botanical shapes were collaged onto a manila folder and texturized with glue. Once the glue dried, the plate was inked with fall colors to create prints, making it beautiful as well.

Collagraph plate

12" W × 12" H (30.48 × 30.48 cm)

Collagraph prints can be used to create sheets of patterned paper, which can then be used to create other art pieces, such as the jewelry pieces shown left. The collagraph print, shown right in the photo, was created from a mix of tag board cutouts, dried glue dots, and other textural pieces. The plate was inked with water-soluble block-printing ink and printed onto text-weight paper. Charms were then cut from the prints and adhered to dominoes and other game pieces.

"Untitled"

Collagraph prints on paper with tiles, game pieces, and jewelry findings

1" W × 1" H (2.54 × 2.54 cm), 1" W × 3" H (2.54 × 7.62 cm), ¾" W × 1½" H (1.905 × 3.81 cm), ¾" W × ¾" H (1.905 × 1.905 cm)

Julie Snidle

This mixed-media collage features a combination of techniques. The large leaves were printed using the collagraph technique while the smaller accents are examples of gelatin monotype prints. The background is a monotype print.

"Untitled"

Collagraph and gelatin monotype prints on monotype background

12" W × 16" H (30.48 × 40.64 cm)

This accordion book features collagraph prints that resemble the city of Jerusalem with lollipops floating above it in the night sky. It signifies childhood memories of holidays in the ancient city—going to Jerusalem was synonymous with holiday parties, candy, and fireworks.

"Lollipops Over Jerusalem"

Collagraph prints on paper

12" W × 6" H × ½" D (30.48 × 15.24 × 1.27 cm)

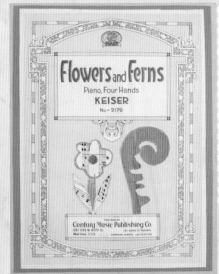

Vibrant collagraph and thermal prints were collaged together on top of painted papers and sheet music in this accordion book. Scraps from the prints were used to create page borders.

"Flowers and Ferns"

Collagraph and thermal prints on painted papers and sheet music

9" W × 12" H (22.86 × 30.48 cm)

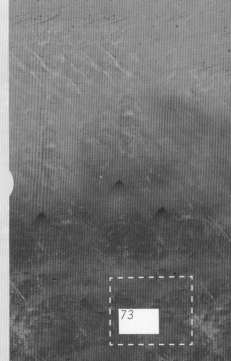

PRINTED PORTRAITS

If you are looking for an interesting and rewarding printmaking challenge, consider creating a portrait with one of the printmaking techniques covered in this book. The human face is a wonderful creative playground, full of opportunities for experimentation. When embarking on a portrait, whether your own or someone else's, think about the effect you wish to achieve. Do you want to create something lifelike or more abstract? Each of the printmaking techniques introduced in this book has a distinctive look. If you wish to create a highly detailed portrait, screen printing with the photo-emulsion process would be your best choice. Screen printing with a paper stencil would be a bolder choice that is still visually accurate. For more graphic and abstract representations, try working with collagraph or relief printing techniques. Monoprinting and screen printing with drawing fluid will help you achieve something softer. Your choice of paper and ink will also effect the final result, so again, experiment, experiment, experiment. The size of your finished print should also be taken into consideration—large prints or large mixed-media pieces can benefit from a richly detailed print, but a postcard-size of the same print could result in some of the detail being lost.

Collagraph prints can create a variety of portraits. This collagraph plate was designed so that, once printed, every facial feature could be cut out and used in different collages. Several prints in several different colors were printed from a single cardboard plate, cut out, and then collaged together.

Collagraph plate

8" W × 8" H (20.32 × 20.32 cm)

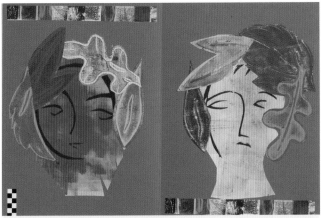

This playful portrait is composed of several collagraph prints that resulted from the collagraph plate on the previous page. Experiment with the cutout facial features to create infinite faces showcasing every mood.

"Untitled"

Collagraph prints on paper

10" W × 12" H (25.4 × 30.48 cm)

These mixed-media printed portraits are part of an accordion book full of contemplative faces. The first layer of each is a monotype print. Then, a paper stencil was used to print the eyes, nose, and mouth. For the hair, several colored leaf cutouts were printed using the collagraph technique and then attached around the face. The decorative border was created from the scraps of the collagraph prints.

"Untitled"

Paper-stencil screen and collagraph prints on paper with collage

9" W × 10" H (22.86 × 25.4 cm)

Experimentation was largely at play during the creation of these two portraits, in which one paper stencil was used to create both. In the first print (left), the stencil was printed first on white paper, then collage elements were cut from a magazine. In the second print (right), the torn magazine page was attached first to the white paper, and the stencil was printed as a second layer.

"Untitled"

Paper stencil screen print on paper with collage

9" W × 10" H (22.86 × 25.4 cm)

For this self portrait, the process started with a paper stencil. When printed, spot color was used to create accents (see page 33). This screen print required five separate stencils and a registration system to assure correct placement of each color.

"Untitled"

Paper-stencil screen print with spot color on paper

9" W × 12" H (22.86 × 30.48 cm)

This piece started with a monoprinted background created with acrylic paint on watercolor paper. The face image was printed using the photo-emulsion technique. The flowers were printed with the collagraph technique and collaged as the final layer.

"Untitled"

Thermal, monoprint, and collagraph prints on paper

12" W × 12" H (30.48 × 30.48 cm)

This piece is a collage using three types of printmaking: the decorative paper framing the image was created using the monotype technique; the apple, leaves, and snake were made with a collagraph plate; and the face was made from a stencil cut from freezer paper and screened onto a map.

"Travels With Eve"

Handcut silkscreen, collagraph, and monotype prints on paper

9" W × 12" H (22.86 × 30.48 cm)

Carol Kemp

The three faces in this mixed-media print are faces of young girls. The smooth lines in the facial features and soft lines reflect youth. To create the screen print, the paper stencils were cut to show faces that are pure, with no wrinkles or signs of stress. They were screen printed on yellow paper and adhered over a blue background, which is a monotype print that symbolizes freshness and open sky. To add to the feminine feel and natural atmosphere, collagraphed flowers and butterflies (cut from a magazine) were added as accents.

"Untitled"

Paper-stencil screen prints on paper with collage

11" W × 16" H (27.94 × 40.64 cm)

This painted wood panel was printed with a thermal screen. To create the screen, the face was hand drawn onto a transparency sheet with an opaque black marker and then burned onto the screen using a thermograph machine. Some paint was added to the edges of the panel to give it an "aged" look.

"Untitled"

Thermal print on painted wood

6" W × 8" H (15.24 × 20.32 cm)

This collection of portraits is part of a fabric book full of printed vintage faces (see pages 104–105 for more details). The background fabric was first dyed with liquid watercolor and tea. The printed faces were created from a thermal screen with brown ink to resemble sepia heirloom photos. The portraits were stitched to the fabric pages and embellished with vintage trims and lace.

"Untitled"

Thermal prints on fabric

8½" W × 11" H × 1" D (21.59 × 27.94 × 2.54 cm)

For this monotype print, the artist used monotype inks to paint a portrait onto an acrylic glass plate. She dampened the paper and then burnished the image onto it. The tulips were collaged and the details filled in with colored pencils.

"Garden Girl"

Monotype print with monotype ink on recycled cotton paper with collage and colored pencils

8" W × 9" H (20 × 22.8 cm)

Laura Ryan

This is a relief print. Battleship linoleum was glued down onto a piece of board to provide a stable plate on which to carve. The shedding of the snake's skin is a symbol of rebirth, resurrection, and rejuvenation.

"Woman With Snakes"

Linoleum-cut relief print on paper

10" W × 8" H (25.54 × 20.32 cm)

Carol Kemp

What is Relief Printing?

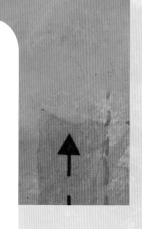

If you are familiar with rubber stamps, then you are familiar with relief printing. Relief printing is a printmaking method in which the inked, raised surfaces of a carved block create an image when pressed to paper. The areas that have been carved do not come into contact with the ink and create the negative space within the design. Relief blocks can be carved from linoleum, cork, erasers, wood, and even styrofoam. Most of the relief prints in this book originated from "soft carving blocks," which are rubbery blocks that are very easy to carve. They are also double-sided. Therefore, if you make a mistake, you can turn the block over and start fresh. In addition to the main carved design, you can also carve texture into the remaining area of the block, such as additional cutout lines and crosshatch, or you can remove all of the remaining area, allowing it to appear blank when printed.

The wood grain in this print was easily revealed. The artist used birch plywood blocks, and before carving them, inked them and printed them to capture the subtle wood grain for the finished print.

"Baby Blue and Yellow Ochre"

Birch-plywood relief prints with oil-based inks on paper

24" W × 24" H (61 × 61 cm)

Annie J. Swincinski

Creating Your Design

As mentioned earlier, relief printing requires the carving of a design onto a block, which is then covered with ink and used to create an impression. Several ways exist to transfer your desired image to the block. Keep in mind that when you print with a relief block, the printed image will be the reverse of the image on the block.

DIRECT FREEHAND DRAWING

Using a soft pencil, you can freehand draw a design onto your block. Mistakes can be easily erased or simply ignored when you are ready to carve.

SOFT-PENCIL METHOD

Use a soft pencil to trace the relief block onto paper. Draw the image that you wish to carve inside the perimeter. Flip the paper over and color in the entire perimeter of the block. Lay the paper image-side up onto the relief block and use a ballpoint pen to trace the design. The image will transfer onto the block by the pressure of the pen on the soft lead. You can also use a soft pencil to draw an image onto paper and then burnish onto the block with your fingers.

CARBON PAPER

Lay your design over carbon paper and place onto the block. Trace the lines of the image with a ballpoint pen.

ACETONE

Place a toner-based copy of your image facedown on the block. Use a small rag dipped into acetone or nail polish remover that contains acetone to burnish the image onto the block. Lift a corner to make sure it is transferring before you remove the paper.

This relief print was created from two carved linoleum blocks. The first block was printed as the background. Then the artist added hand-torn natural papers before printing the second block.

"Sunrise Ginkos"

Linoleum-block relief print with oil-based inks on paper

6" W × 8" H (15 × 20.25 cm)

Annie J. Swincinski

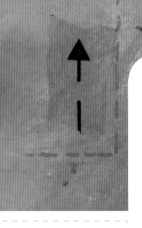

Basic
Relief Printing

When creating a relief print, the first thing you will want to do is create the block. Choose a design—as you become accustomed to the carving tools, opt for a design with simple shapes and broad lines. Next, choose a block to carve. Styrofoam is a great starter block because it is easy to carve (a dull pencil or ball-point pen will do the trick) and inexpensive (you can use recycled styrofoam packaging from the super-market). Plus, styrofoam is flexible, so you can print on surfaces that are not flat. For ink, you can use printing inks or rubber-stamping inks, which you can apply directly to your block by tapping the ink pad right on the block. When you are finished, wipe the block clean with a damp cloth and allow to dry.

The collection of images below were printed onto fabric with the relief-printing technique. Designs were carved into school erasers, which were then inked and pressed onto the fabric.

"Untitled"

Eraser-cut relief prints on fabric

8" W × 10" H (20.32 × 25.4 cm)

Pati Bristow

TECHNIQUE

1 Sketch your design on a piece of paper with a soft pencil.

2 To transfer the image to the block, lay the sheet on top of the block with the image facing the block. Use your finger to burnish the image onto the block. Lift a corner of the paper to make sure your image is transferred before you remove it.

3 Decide whether you wish to print the positive or negative image. For the positive image, use carving tools to carve out the background areas of the image; for the negative image, carve out the main image.

materials

Paper • Soft pencil • Eraser, linoleum, cork, styrofoam, etc., for carving • Carving tools • Water-based block-printing ink • Brayer • Acrylic glass or glass plate • Assortment of thin papers

4 Apply an even coat of ink to the brayer and roll the brayer over the carved block. Cover the block with a thin, even layer of ink. Lay a piece of paper over the inked block and burnish with the pillow of your hand.

5 Pull the paper to reveal the print. If the design would benefit from more definition, wipe the ink off of the block and recarve as needed.

This print is a combination of techniques, including drawn elements, mini-silkscreen Gocco printing, and elements from prior wood block prints.

"Collage 17"

Silkscreen Gocco and wood-block prints on canvas with drawing

6" W × 6" H (15.24 × 15.24 cm)

Marissa L. Swinghammer

This print on Japanese paper was created from various relief prints cut from wooden blocks.

"Black Purple Dragonfly"

Relief print on Japanese paper

6" W × 6" H (15.24 × 15.24 cm)

Marissa L. Swinghammer

This hybrid of prints features a variety of wood-block relief prints as well as tea-soaked Japanese paper and Chyrogami washi paper.

"Collage 12"

Wood-block relief prints on Japanese and Chyrogami washi paper with collage

6" W × 6" H (15.24 × 15.24 cm)

Marissa L. Swinghammer

This print features a wood-block print of a girl on top of a monotype print.

"Mysterious Stranger"

Wood-block relief and monotype prints on canvas

6" W × 6" H (15.24 × 15.24 cm)

Marissa L. Swinghammer

What is Sun Printing?

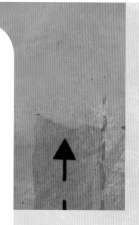

If you are intrigued by darkroom photography, then this technique, which relies on the photographic process, will certainly spur your creativity. Sun printing, also known as cyanotype process and blueprint process, is a photographic method of printing using the sun (or a UV light source) for transferring the image to fabric or paper. It is inexpensive, easy, and relatively nontoxic. You will need a dark room for this technique—you can cover windows with black fabric or trash bags if necessary.

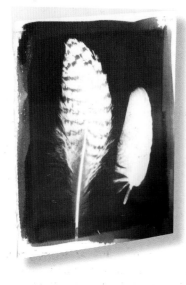

The sun prints on these handmade cards were created by layering feathers and Japanese maple leaves onto a transparency and then onto watercolor paper treated with cyanotype solution. The materials were exposed in the sun for a few minutes and then the papers were rinsed and allowed to dry.

Sun prints on watercolor paper, botanicals, feathers

5" W × 7" H (12.7 × 17.78 cm), 4" W × 5" H (10.16 × 12.7 cm)

Linda Stinchfield

Vintage correspondence and botanicals are the subjects of the sun prints featured in this handmade accordion book. To print the correspondence, first scan and print onto a transparency. Cover a sheet of paper treated with cyanotype solution with the transparency and expose in sunlight to achieve the desired effect.

"Even Teasles Get the Blues"

Sun prints on paper, corrugated card stock, botanicals, vintage correspondence, porcupine quill

40" W × 7¾ " H (101.6 × 19.69 cm)

Linda Stinchfield

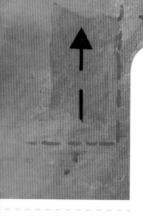

Basic
Sun Printing

When choosing images to print with this technique, opt for black opaque images or dimensional objects that will not allow light to pass through them. This will result in a nice, sharp print, instead of a pale or fuzzy image that could occur with a more detailed choice. Besides the sun and your printing materials, one of the main ingredients you will need to complete this technique successfully is a dark room for prepping. All of the prep work will be completed in this room, so any drying of materials prior to moving out into the sun will need to occur here as well. If you choose to store your project before printing, keep it inside a drawer or black heavy plastic bag. When transporting your printing materials from the dark room to the sunlight area, be careful not to disturb the paper and image. Secure the materials from unwanted wind movement since movement will result in a blurry print. Cover the materials with a heavy piece of glass, or you can pin or tape the perimeters. Place the printing materials in a spot that receives direct sunlight without the obstruction of shadows from trees, fences, etc. The quality of light will determine the exposure time—sunny days will require less exposure time than cloudy days. To find the best exposure time, test a small piece of paper or fabric ahead of time.

Preparing the Cyanotype Solution

Although you can prepare the cyanotype solution necessary for this technique from scratch, the two solutions necessary to create the printing solution—Solution A: Potassium Ferricyanide and Solution B: Ferric Ammonium Citrate—are readily available and only require mixing in equal amounts. Prepare only the appropriate amount for your project as the mixed solution will be good only for a few days. The leftover Solutions A and B should remain separate in bottles that will not allow light to penetrate them. Protect your working area since the cyanotype solution can stain any surface it touches, and wear protective gloves and work clothes.

TECHNIQUE

1

Objects with a sharp outline such as plants, leaves, or feathers • Transparency • Paper or natural fiber fabric that has been washed to remove sizing • Dark room • Cyanotype solution or pretreated fabric or paper • Paintbrush • Designated area with direct sunlight and free from shadows • Two plastic containers (size should accommodate the treated paper/fabric) filled with tap water • Piece of wood, a sheet of glass, and a piece of foam sized slightly larger than the paper/fabric you are going to print on

1. In a dark room, prepare the cyanotype solution according to the directions on page 88. Brush the solution onto your chosen printing surface—brush first in one direction and then repeat in the perpendicular direction, making sure the entire area is evenly covered. If working with a large piece of fabric, dip it into the solution and lightly wring it out.

2

2. Prepare a support for the paper or fabric by stacking a piece of foam on top of a piece of wood—both should be at least as big as the paper or fabric. Place the paper or fabric on top of the support and smooth out any wrinkles in the fabric. If working with paper, make sure the paper is completely dry; if working with fabric, you can proceed wet or dry.

3

3. Place the transparency with the black image(s) on top of your paper or fabric and top with glass to create a tight seal. If using heavier dimensional objects, the glass won't be necessary. Being careful to keep the project still, transfer it to an area that receives direct sunlight. Make sure that the area will not be affected by shadows throughout the day.

4. Monitor the project for color change. The sun is a catalyst for a chemical reaction causing the yellow solution to change to green and then to blue, leaving the images shaded from the sun white. If printing on dry fabric, the color change will be subtle. Therefore, it is best to time the reaction. This process should last a few minutes.

4

5   Once the reaction is complete, remove the glass and transparency or dimensional objects. Soak the paper or fabric in a container of water for a few minutes (best to prepare ahead of time), constantly moving it with a gloved hand. When the water turns dark green, transfer the paper or fabric to a container of fresh water and continue to soak. Allow for a ten-minute rinse while moving it with your hand every few minutes. When finished, dilute the water in a large bucket and dispose of it.

6   Remove the paper or fabric from the water and lay flat to dry away from direct sunlight.

Sun prints will always print blue. Here the leaf image was printed on a box painted light blue for a lovely monochromatic effect. Blue fibers and dried white botanicals emphasize the light blue print on the background.

"Beach House"

Sun print on painted found wooden boxes with dimensional collage and fibers

10" W × 10" H × 1" D (25.4 × 25.4 × 2.54 cm)

Exposing a sun print should only take two or three minutes. If you pull the print too soon it will be light; if you leave it out too long, it will be dark. These images were first copied onto a transparency using the black-and-white/reverse function and then printed on paper.

"Sanity Is a Fluid"

Sun prints on paper

5½" W × 7¾" H × ¾" D (14 × 20.5 × 2 cm)

Rae Trujillo

going on forever
without
going anywhere

inhabiting
a
strange world.

ed from that dizzy height, the narrow sheet of the "holy lake," i
lands. At the distance of a few leagues, the bed of the waters b
along their bosom, before a light morning air. But a narrow op
ll further north, to spread their pure and ample sheets again, b
le, or rather broken plain, so often mentioned. For several mile
e level and sandy lands, across which we have accompanied ou
osite sides of the lake and valley, clouds of light vapor were risi
ges; or rolled lazily down the declivities, to mingle with the frogs
spot beneath which lay the silent pool of the pond. Directly on

chapter four

Mixed-Media **Printing Projects**

ADD PRINTMAKING TO YOUR ARTISTIC PROCESS TO CREATE UNIQUE PIECES

Your training in elementary printmaking techniques has been achieved. Now, you can build on your techniques by using them as a basis for mixed-media art creations. As you have learned, printmaking is a process, a journey. The first step can be taken somewhat timidly—the ground may be unfamiliar. But, the reward will be exquisite. It is important to trust in the process in order to be successful as a mixed-media printmaker. The projects that follow demonstrate the transformation of a regular art print into a mixed-media print. Rarely are these creations executed in just one sitting. Again, mixed-media printmaking is a process. Some days the mixed-media printmaker just makes prints and on other days, she sews, collages, and makes books. As you endeavor, take the steps at your own pace and enjoy watching the journey unfold.

The Creative Process

If you're ready to begin mixed-media printmaking but not sure where to start, here is a step-by-step plan. Creating mixed-media art with prints is definitely a process. Trust the process and move through it in a way that is personally inspiring to you.

Choose Your Theme

The first step to creating a work of art is focusing on a central theme. Your theme can come from anywhere, such as a trip you recently took, nature, the seasons, a beautiful landscape, or a loved one. Begin to think about the type of feeling you want your prints to evoke and jot down some notes and ideas. Once you settle on a theme, you'll need to find imagery. Imagery can be your own photograph, a copyright-free image in a book, or your own original drawing. Start a collection so that you have options.

Consider the Size

In your mind's eye, how large is the final piece? Is it very large or very small? Remember, the size of your print will affect the amount of detail visible to the human eye. If you want a large print with a lot of detail, consider using the screen-print photo-emulsion process. For a more graphic look, opt for collagraph or relief printing.

The colors and subject matter on this collagraph plate impart an ethereal, heavenly, even majestic feel. Take a few moments to pair your imagery with appropriate colors for artwork that truly shines.

Collagraph plate

12" W × 12" H (30.48 × 30.48 cm)

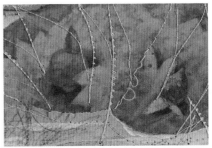

The theme of this mixed-media collage centers around the three young girls in the piece, who are all named after flowers. The background contains botanical prints symbolic of the girls' names. The print of the young girls is a drawing-fluid and screen-filler screen print. To create the print, the image of the girls was traced onto a transparency from a photograph. The tracing was used to then create the screen print, which made the resulting print look more like a drawing.

"Three Flowers"

Drawing-fluid and screen-filler screen print on paper with recycled calendar page, scraps of old prints, stitching, fabric scraps

11" W × 14" H (27.94 × 35.56 cm)

Choose Your Technique, Substrate, and Ink

You have a theme and you know the tone you wish to convey. With that in mind, choose a suitable technique, substrate, and ink appropriate for the theme and tone. When choosing a substrate, consider printing on a variety of materials so that you have several variations to choose from. Fabric scraps, plain paper, lightly textured paper, painted paper, torn book pages . . . the possibilities are endless.

Print

Gather your supplies, set up your workspace, and begin printing. Remember that printmaking, just like any new acquired skill, requires practice. Do not be discouraged if your first attempts are not successful. Just be inspired by the images, the colors, the textures, and the possibilities that await you.

Compose

Decide on a background for your mixed-media art and start playing. Arrange the prints so that the resulting composition is unified and balanced. Begin by choosing a focal point and then support pieces. Alter the prints by tearing the edges, cutting out vignettes, or adding other media to them. Seek opportunities to create rhythm in your composition. For example, place several small collagraphed cutouts around the focal point of your print.

Commit

Once you have your primary composition laid out you'll need to secure them temporarily. You can use a bit of glue (from a glue stick) or pin them with sewing pins. At this point, it might be wise to allow the piece to rest for a bit. Return after a few hours to see if you still like your original composition. If so, proceed to secure it permanently. Otherwise, continue to experiment. If you are ready to adhere the pieces, there are two different ways to do so:

SEWING Stitching will add more texture and detail to the piece. Whether you use handstitching or machine stitching, try alternating between straight and zigzag stitches. Use a free-motion foot if you have one. If your piece is large, try dividing it into a few smaller sections. Once finished, you can secure them together with thread.

GLUING If you prefer to glue the components, use the appropriate glue. For delicate paper, use a glue stick or matte gel medium. Regular craft glue can be used for heavier stock. Wet glues have a tendency to cause paper to curl, so use a heavy object to keep the paper flat during drying. Keep in mind that unsealed water-based inks, except for acrylics, will smear if they get wet; avoid brushing glue on the tops of such prints. As an alternative, an adhesion-application machine can be purchased at relatively low cost. Feed paper through these machines, and they will apply a thin, even coat of adhesive to the back. When working with fabrics, opt for fabric glue, using the bare minimum and being careful to smooth out any wrinkles that may appear.

Finish

All that is left are the finishing touches. This is the point where you add any embellishments or additional texture that will help completely unify the piece. This stage presents another opportunity to walk away from the piece for a while. When you return, re-examine the piece for overall balance. Would either side benefit from more visual weight? Try adding another collaged layer with a printed piece. Are the colors in harmony? If not, try adding fiber scraps, a bit of paint, or some rubber stamping. If the piece cries out for texture, consider adding stitching, buttons, beads, or trim. Another fun finishing option is to print over a print or over a collage. You can screen print over any surface (printed, collaged, stitched, etc.) as long as it is relatively smooth. You can also use your carved blocks or erasers just like you would use rubber stamps and stamp over your print or collage.

Save

Once you are finished with your creation, collect the scraps and unused pieces and squirrel them away for your next project. Perhaps you have leftover prints that were not your favorite. Don't throw them away in haste. They could be the perfect complement to a yet-to-be-conceived creation.

This collage was created entirely from scrap prints and scrap wallpaper. Always save your leftover materials, whether they are prints, scraps of paper or fabric, or found objects.

"In the Field"

Collagraph print on wallpaper with colored pencil

18" W × 12" H (45.72 × 30.48 cm)

Printmaking **Projects**

Now that you have learned several printmaking techniques, it is time to go a step further and incorporate them into mixed-media works of art. What follows are nine mixed-media projects, each one featuring one of the printmaking techniques shown previously. Review the projects to see how much creativity printmaking can add to your creative endeavors. The projects can be re-created or serve as a springboard for your own original masterpieces. Also, please don't hesitate to use different printmaking techniques with the projects than those shown here.

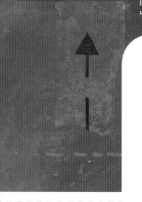

Three Sisters

In this piece, three sisters were created using the paper-stencil screen-printing technique described on pages 30–31 as well as the collagraph printing technique on pages 68–69. Screen printing with paper stencils is one of the easiest printmaking techniques to master. The trickiest part is understanding the reverse-image factor—you need to be sure that when you attach the paper stencil to the screen-printing frame, you attach it so that it is the mirror image of your desired finished print. But, when you are working with faces, it won't matter if you mess up because it only affects the direction of the eyes and nose. When choosing this technique, keep in mind that you'll have more success with larger, simpler shapes than those that are smaller with fine details.

materials

White and colored copy paper
• Craft knife • Scissors • Black marker • Masking tape • Screen-printing frame • Squeegee • Screen-printing ink • Pencil • Manila folder or card stock • Glue • Block-printing ink • Water-soluble crayons or watercolor paint • Watercolor paper
• Found paper • Fabric scraps
• Ephemera

15" W × 20" H (38.1 × 50.8 cm)

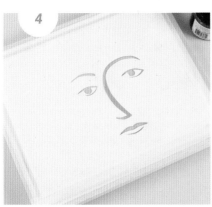

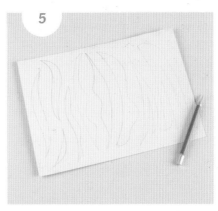

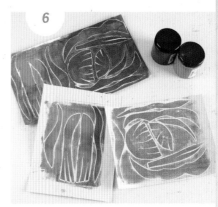

4   To print the faces, attach the stencil to the outside of the screen-printing frame. Use screen-printing ink to print all of the faces onto the painted watercolor paper (see pages 30–31 for detailed instructions). Allow to dry and rinse the screen thoroughly.

5   Draw hair styles onto a piece of cardboard or a recycled manila folder. Cut out the shapes and attach to another piece of cardboard, recycled manila folder, or piece of heavy paper.

6   Print the hair using the collagraph printing technique (see pages 68–69 for detailed instructions) and block-printing ink. Allow to dry and place under a stack of heavy books to flatten.

7   Once all of the prints are dry, cut them out and begin to collage them together. Embellish the piece with found paper, fabric scraps, and other pieces of ephemera.

1   Use watercolor paints or water-soluble crayons to paint a color wash onto two sheets of watercolor paper. Choose a wash suitable for skin tone and another for the background. Allow to dry completely and place under a stack of heavy books to flatten.

2   Draw a set of faces on paper with black marker and mark the areas you wish to print by coloring them in.

3   Create paper stencils by using a craft knife to cut out the marked areas.

Dimensional Assemblage

As long as a surface is relatively flat and smooth, it's a prime candidate for screen printing. Therefore, don't be deterred from printing on dimensional items, such as the wooden boxes used in this project. This project showcases three different printing techniques on wood: The bird motif was printed using the drawing-fluid and screen-filler screen-printing technique shown on pages 38–39; the background script was printed with the thermal-screen-printing process shown on pages 52–53; and the leaves were printed with the gelatin monotype technique shown on pages 64–65. When printing on wood, screen printing and sun printing will likely result in the sharpest prints. For sun prints, opt for wood that is very smooth and light in color, and the resulting blue print will have a nice contrast. If you wish to incorporate collagraph or monotype prints onto a wooden piece, it would be best to print the images onto paper or fabric and then attach them to the piece.

materials

Wooden boxes in an assortment of sizes • Wooden panels • Stretched canvas • Acrylic paint • Paintbrush • Drawing fluid • Screen filler • Thermal-imaging printer • Thermal-imaging screens • Screen-printing ink • Screen-printing frame • Squeegee • Gelatin • Shallow pan • Block-printing ink • Collage elements (two- and three-dimensional) • Heavy-duty adhesive

24" W × 18" H × 2" D (60.96 × 45.72 × 5.08 cm)

1 Gather wooden boxes in different sizes and shapes as well as a few smaller wooden panels and one large wooden panel. The largest panel or box will serve as the base. Choose a background color and paint all of the boxes and panels.

2 Choose your images and patterns to print onto the boxes and panels. Add any flat collage elements to the boxes and panels prior to printing (you can add more after the prints have dried, too).

3 Print the images and patterns directly onto the wooden surfaces. Alternate the ink colors as desired. When printing patterns, if your screen is too small for the area you want to cover, print the pattern more then once to cover the area. Let each area dry completely before you print on or next to it. You may use registration marks if you desire clear and sharp prints.

4 When the printed areas dry, attach the small boxes to the large one using heavy-duty adhesive.

5 Add another layer of paint and painted highlights. Smear the paint with your finger or wipe some of it off. Add dimensional decorative elements, such as wood, fabric, foam, buttons, etc. Seal the piece by brushing it with gel medium in matte finish.

Iconic
Screen-Print Collage

To many people, Andy Warhol is synonymous with screen printing. This piece was created as a tribute to his graphic and boldly colorful prints of Hollywood icons. The image of Ann Sheridan (photographed by George Hurrell, 1939) was photocopied from a book of copyright-free images. If you enjoy using photos in your art, projects such as this are a perfect opportunity to do so. Scrapbook artists may find that this is an opportunity to expand on their photo techniques, and, in fact, the card stock used for the prints is common scrapbooking paper. To print these images, the screen printing with photographic-emulsion process explained on pages 48–49 was used. When working with this technique, the challenge is spreading the photo-emulsion solution on the screen. As an alternative, the thermal-screen-printing technique on pages 52–52 could be used to create a similar result.

materials

High-contrast portrait photo • Clear transparency • Photo-emulsion solution • Photo-emulsion trough or wide ruler (use for smaller screen) • Dark room • Light source • Screen-printing frame • Squeegee • Screen-printing ink • Brightly colored paper • Card stock

24" W × 24" H (60.96 × 60.96 cm)

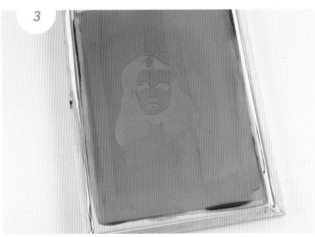

1   Print or copy a high-contrast photographic image in black and white and crop as desired. Ensure that the facial features retain some detail.

2   Print or copy the image onto a transparency.

3   Use the photo-emulsion technique shown on pages 48–49 to burn the image to a screen. Print the image onto four sheets of paper in a variety of colors. Crop the prints so that they are all the same size.

4   Overprint with a different color on one of the prints. The second print should be about 1/16"–1/8" (2–3 mm) off the registration to create the effect shown above. Mat the prints and, if desired, screen print patterns on the borders. Arrange all the prints as desired and attach to a large background to create your final collage.

Tea Party With My Ancestors
Fabric Book

Thermal-imaging printing can be quite addicting. Here, it was used to create a series of prints for a fabric book. Copyright-free illustrations with vintage and Victorian figures were printed onto cotton fabric, but real images of family members and loved ones could be used as well. Book artists are always on the lookout for new and unusual materials to serve as pages in a book. For this project, vintage fabric placemats were repurposed. Those who enjoy sewing will love the quaint embellishments on the pages, which are full of fabric scraps and trims. If you create a similar book with family photos, consider using scraps of old clothing or other heirloom ephemera as accents. The resulting book will be a treasured keepsake for generations to come.

8½" W × 11" H × 1" D
(21.59 × 27.94 × 2.54 cm)

materials

Six fabric placemats or six sheets of fabric trimmed to the same size • ½ yard of white or off-white cotton fabric • Images of men and women (either photographs or line drawings) • Screen-printing ink • Screen-printing frame (traditional or thermal imaging) • Photo-emulsion solution and supplies (if not using thermal-imaging printer) • Needle and thread • Sewing machine • Scissors • Scraps of fabrics, lace, trims, buttons • Tea, coffee, or liquid watercolor paints for staining

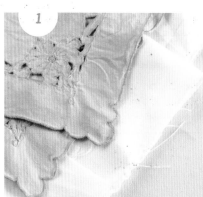

1 Determine the number of pages for the book and gather enough fabric to create the pages. Each piece of fabric will create two pages of the book. This book has ten pages, plus front and back covers, so six pieces of fabric were necessary. Trim the fabric to the desired book size. Dye or stain the fabric using solutions made from tea, coffee, and diluted liquid watercolor paints. Allow the fabric to dry.

2 Choose enough images for the entire book and the covers. This book has ten pages plus a front and back cover, therefore twelve images were chosen.

3 Transfer the images to a screen using either the thermal-screen-printing technique (see pages 52–53) or the photo-emulsion screen-printing technique (see pages 48–49).

4 Screen print all of the images with dark brown ink onto a new piece of light-colored cotton fabric using the technique on pages 52–53. Allow them to dry.

5 Trim the printed images and stitch them to the fabric that will be used to create the pages and cover of the book.

Embellish the fabric with lace, fiber scraps, and trims. Add beads, buttons, and other found objects.

6 Machine stitch the pages back to back leaving an open edge in the middle of the fold area. Insert a piece of card stock or flannel into the opening to stabilize the pages and stitch the opening closed. Stitch the middle section of all folded placemats together to create one block of pages.

7 To prepare the cover, trim one of the fabric sheets up the vertical middle. Measure the spine and find a piece of lace, trim, or fabric in the corresponding size. Place the piece between the front and back covers and sew along the edges to connect them.

8 Wrap the cover around the book and stitch it to the first and last pages of the book. Use a needle and thread to loosely stitch the cover to the spine.

Monotype
Print Journal

This project is perfect for those who appreciate the simple, playful side of creating. It also is a perfect opportunity to start experimenting with monotype printing. The simple color washes and textures will allow you to test the process of pulling a print from an inked plate. You can work with different inks and colorants and also experiment with the amount you put on the plate. You should try different brushes and brayers when applying the ink to the plate. When you select papers, keep in mind that some may need to be dampened or soaked in order to absorb the ink. Test a swatch before beginning. Once you master washes and textures, you can move on to simple images. For a further challenge, try screen printing interesting borders on the journal cover and pages. Once the pages and cover are printed, reach for your stack of test prints and use them to create collages on the inside of the journal. The journal shown here features a pamphlet-stitch binding. As an alternative, simply use a nice ribbon to wrap around the center crease of the open journal. This will hold the pages together and allow free use of the journal.

materials

Assortment of heavy, non-sized papers (such as watercolor papers, card stock, or bristol paper) • Mono-print inks, acrylic paints, and/or pasty watercolor paint • Acrylic glass or glass plate • Brayer • Paintbrushes • Spray bottle • Awl • Waxed linen thread • Embroidery needle

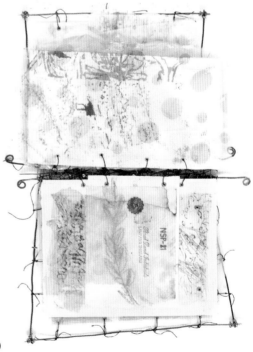

8" W × 10" H × ½" D (20.32 × 25.4 × 1.27 cm)

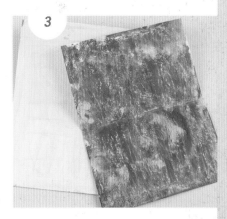

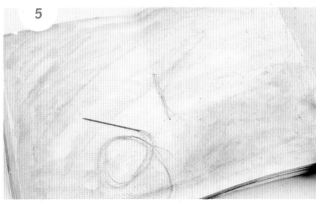

1 Gather papers to print on, such as watercolor paper, textured paper, and bristol paper. For a tidy journal, trim all of the papers to the same size.

2 Prepare a plate to accommodate the largest piece of paper in your collection with monoprint inks, acrylic paints, or pasty watercolors. Lay the paper on the inked plate and burnish with the pillow of your hand. Remove the paper and allow it to dry flat.

3 Once the papers are dry, use watercolors to create a wash on the back side of the papers and allow to dry. Place under a stack of heavy books to flatten.

4 Gather ten printed papers, fold them in half, and arrange into one signature. Include found papers if desired.

5 Using an awl, punch a hole in the middle of the center crease through all of the papers. Punch a second and third hole an inch above and an inch below the first. Use waxed linen thread and an embroidery needle to create a pamphlet stitch. Tie the ends in a knot and trim the excess.

Gelatin
Monotype Placemats

Gelatin monotype prints are so fun to create. The gelatin plate has such a funky look and feel, it makes you just want to play with it. There are also so many creative possibilities. Fibers were laid onto a gelatin plate to create the texture on these placemats, but any number of materials could be used, such as paper cutouts, textured papers, or flower petals. The gelatin will take a few hours to set, therefore prepare the gelatin a day in advance and store it in the refrigerator. When choosing a shallow pan for the gelatin, you can either use a pan that is large enough to accommodate the entire size of the placemats, or you can use a smaller pan and print the mats in sections. These mats were created with a small shallow pan. Several small prints were pulled and then two or three were stitched together to create each placemat.

materials

Assortment of textured fibers, ribbons, and trims • Six to eight pieces of copy paper 17" W × 11" H • Block-printing ink in a variety of colors • Brayer • Acrylic or glass plate • Gelatin • Shallow pan • Laminate sheets

17" W × 11" H (43.18 × 27.94 cm)

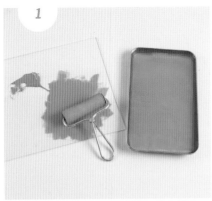

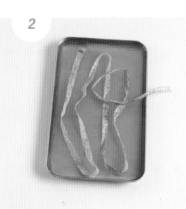

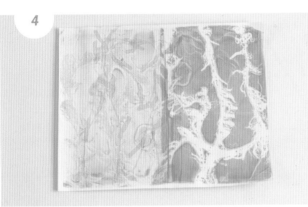

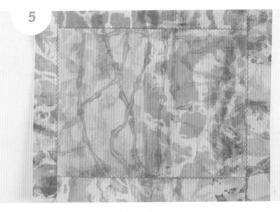

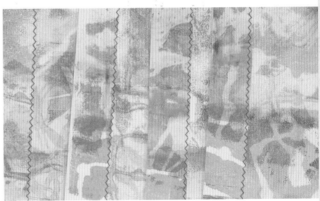

1   Use a brayer to spread a small amount of ink onto a glass plate. Brayer an even coat of ink onto the gelatin.

2   Place fibers onto the gelatin in a random pattern.

3   Print a positive and then a negative print of the design onto paper using the instructions on pages 64–65. Repeat for the rest of your placemats, changing colors and patterns as desired.

4   Begin layering new printed designs on the previous prints, using a new color of ink. Be careful not to completely overprint. Allow all the prints to dry.

5   Combine a few prints so that once attached you will have 17" W × 11" H (43 × 28 cm) sheets. Attach with glue or stitching. Continue embellishing as desired. Once satisfied, laminate the placemats, leaving a 1/8" (3 mm) border around the print.

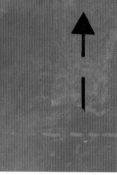

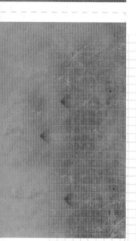

Holiday
Flag Book

This flag book is fun because it has an element of surprise. Here, a holiday theme was used, but you can alter the theme to fit any occasion. Collagraph prints are fun and easy ways to create bold and graphic prints. Therefore, the collagraph technique is suitable for art when a clear image is required. Have fun with inks when creating collagraph prints. Solid-color prints are great, but a mix of colors is also easy to create. You also can effortlessly add texture to your collagraph prints—on the project below, glue dots were added to the letters to create a grainy effect. Because this project requires printed text, take extra care to ensure your finished print will read correctly.

materials

One sheet of 8½" W × 10" H white card stock • Eight 2½" W × 2½" H squares of green card stock • Seven 2½" W × 2½" H squares of red card stock • Two pieces of 6¼" W × 8½" H decorative paper • Manila folder or card stock • Glue stick • Scissors • Block-printing ink • Brayer • Acrylic glass or glass plate • Decorative trim

8½" W × 2⅝" H (21.59 × 6.7 cm) (closed)

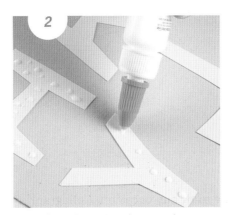

1 Create an accordion fold by alternately folding a strip of paper. This book was folded nine times from an 8½" W × 10" H (21.5 × 25.5 cm) sheet of card stock. Cut eight 2½" W × 2½" H (6.5 × 6.5 cm) squares from green card stock and seven from red card stock.

2 Trim the letters from a recycled manila folder or card stock so that they are about 2" W × 2" H (5 × 5 cm) and cut out a hyphen as well. Glue the letters and hyphen to a piece of card stock. Texturize the letters by adding dots of white glue directly on top of them. Allow the glue to dry.

3 Use the collagraph-printing technique on pages 68–69 to print the letters four times—twice on white paper with red ink and twice on white paper with green ink. Allow to dry.

4 Trim the letters and hyphens and attach the red letters to the green cardboard squares and vice versa. Attach the squares to the accordion book in three rows with each row alternating in direction.

5 To create the cover for the book, cut two pieces of 8½" W × 6¼" H (21.5 × 16 cm) matching color cardboard paper. Add a decorative element to both pieces using screen printing or any other decorative technique. Fold 1" (2.5 cm) of each of these pieces to be attached under the first and last folds of the accordion, and the rest will be folded in half to create two covers.

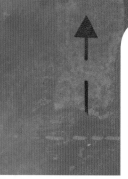

Bless This House

The hand motif and the color turquoise in this relief print are symbols of good luck in Mediterranean culture. Because of its simple shape, the hand is a perfect subject for a relief print. Carving designs can be tricky for an untrained hand, therefore choosing a bold design absent of fine detail and sharp curves would be wise. To practice, carve some shapes onto a small eraser first. Don't let the carving intimidate you because for this project, you will use a block made from a softer material, making it easy to maneuver a carving tool through it. If you make a mistake, you can turn the block over and start fresh. As you carve, orient your work so that you are carving away from your body.

materials

Paper • Soft pencil • Black paper
• Soft carving block • Carving tools
• An old manila folder or a scrap of
paper with similar weight • Glue
• Silver block-printing ink • Scissors
• Alphabet rubber stamps • Mat
board or cardboard painted with silver
paint • Wire or ribbon • Rhinestones
• Accent stickers

8" W × 10" H (20.32 × 25.4 cm)

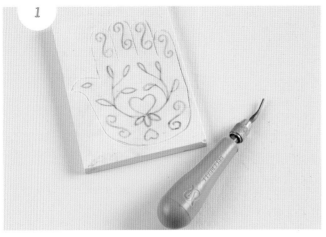

1 Draw or copy the hand motif onto paper and transfer it to a linoleum block. Carve out the design and, if desired, create a pattern on the remaining background.

2 Print the design with silver ink onto black paper.

3 Use the collagraph-printing technique on pages 68–69 to create a mat for the print in the shape of a house. Stamp the phrase "bless this house" onto the top of the new print.

4 If necessary, trim the first print to fit onto the mat and adhere it to the mat with glue. Adhere this to a sturdy background and embellish with rhinestones and stickers. Attach a ribbon hanger to the top.

Sun-Kissed
Fabric Wall Hanging

If you ever feel guilty about spending the day in your creative space when it is bright and sunny, this project will remedy that—sun printing is very much an indoor/outdoor activity. But it does require some planning. First, you need to check the weather to find a suitable calm day. Sunny days are great, but you need to be mindful of shadows. Overcast days will provide more even light, but exposure time will be longer. Next, designate a temporary dark room and a dark place to store the treated paper or fabric prior to exposure. Finally, plan your workspace setup and your disposal process. Now that you have gone through all of this work, why not enjoy a full-blown sun-printing session? Otherwise, it would be terrible to go through all this work for just one print!

materials

Cyanotype solution • Dark room • Designated location with direct sunlight and no shadows • Sheet of glass, block of wood, piece of foam for support • Two squares of fabric • Scraps of lace, trims, and fabrics in matching colors • Sewing machine • Long-stem flowers and plants (real or artificial) • Brunch

14" W × 40" H (35.56 × 101.6 cm)

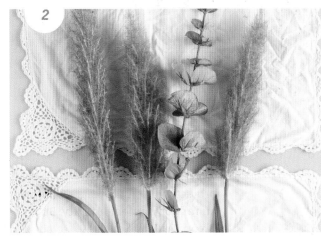

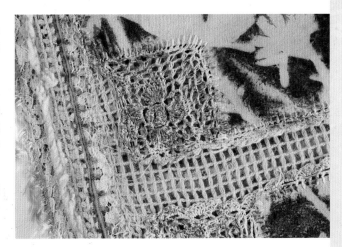

1   Prepare two pieces of fabric, such as two blank fabric napkins, for sun printing according to the steps on pages 86–87.

2   Position the fabric pieces so that they lie next to one another but do not overlap. Place the stems on top of the fabric so that they touch both pieces. Use the sun-printing technique on pages 86–87 to print on the fabric. Allow the fabric to dry.

3   Place the fabric pieces on top of a larger fabric background and embellish with fabric scraps. Stitch all of the components in place and add decorative trim.

4   Flip the artwork over and stitch a sleeve or loops to the top. Insert a brunch or bent wire to hold the wall hanging.

Resources

MANUFACTURERS AND RETAILERS

Blue Prints on Fabric
20504 81st Ave.
Vashon Island, WA 98070
(800) 631-3369
blueprintsonfabric.com
Solutions for sun printing as well as pre-treated paper and fabric

Dharma Trading Co.
PO Box 150916
San Rafael, CA 94915
(800) 542-5227
dharmatrading.com
Esteemed retail outlet for different brands of screen-printing ink and tools for printing on fabric, instructional material, as well as pretreated paper and fabric for sun printing

Dick Blick Art Materials
PO Box 1267
Galesburg, IL 61402-1267
(800) 828-4548
dickblick.com
Block- and screen-printing inks, carving tools, relief blocks, frames, photo-emulsion solution, and exposure units

Graphic Chemical & Ink Co.
732 North Yale Ave.
Villa Park, IL 60181
(630) 832-6004
graphicchemical.com
Relief, screen-printing, and monoprint inks, tools for relief printing, screen printing, and monoprinting

KIWO Inc.
1929 Marvin Cir.
Seabrook, TX 77586
(800) KIWO-USA
kiwo.com
Photo emulsion, photo-emulsion cleaning solution

Nasco
901 Janesville Ave.
Fort Atkinson, WI 53538
(800) 558-9595
enasco.com/artsandcrafts
Block and monoprint printing inks, carving tools, blocks, pretreated paper for sun printing

Daniel Smith Inc.
PO Box 84268
Seattle, WA 98124-5568
(800) 426-7923
danielsmith.com
Relief and monoprint inks, blocks, and carving tools

Speedball
2301 Speedball Rd.
Statesville, NC 28677
(800) 898-7224
speedballart.com
Block- and screen-printing inks, blocks, drawing fluid, screen filler, frames, squeegees, photo-emulsion solution, speed cleaner, instructional material, kits

THERMOGRAPH SUPPLIES

Dorit Elisha
doritelisha.com
For custom-burned screens

Marcy Tilton
marcytilton.com
For custom-burned screens

Welsh Products Inc. (WPI)
1316 Oak Cir.
Arnold, CA 95223
welshproducts.com
Thermograph machines, mesh, frames, inks, instructional media

Bibliography and Additional Reading

Printmaking Techniques by Julia Ayres (Watson-Guptill Publications, 1993)

Screen Printing: The Complete Water-based System by Robert Adam and Carol Robertson (Thames & Hudson, 2003)

Monotype Mediums and Methods for Painterly Printmaking by Julia Ayres (Watson-Guptill Publications, 1991)

Making Monotypes Using a Gelatin Plate by Nancy Marculewicz (Hand Books Press, 2002)

Printmaking by Harvey Daniels (The Viking Press, 1971)

Printmaking for Beginners by Jane Stobart (Watson-Guptill Publications, 2005)

Blueprints on Fabric: Innovative Uses for Cyanotype by Barbara Hewitt (Interweave, 1995)

Printmaking Without a Press by Janet Erickson and Adelaide Sproul (Van Nostrand Reinhold Company, 1966)

Relief Printmaking by Ann Westley (Watson-Guptill Publications, 2002)

Learn to Print Step-by-Step by Bruce Robertson and David Gormley (Macdonald & Co. Publishers Ltd., 1987)

The Book of Alternative Photographic Processes by Christopher James (Delmar/Cengage Learning, 2nd edition, 2008)

"How to Keep Your Studio a Safe Environment" by Daniel Smith, http://www.danielsmith.com/Articles/Healthy-Safe-Studio.asp

Contributing Artists

Artist credits for the Tortilla Curtain Project prints on pages 42–47
Terry Acebo Davis, Jose Arenas, Sheila Baptist, Becky Barber, Daniela Barnea, John Betts, Pati Bristow, Sandra Delman, Dorit Elisha, Yin Yin Hung, Yukari Lassange, Cindy Lee, Kent Manske, Gene Torchia, Tom Wacha, Peter Wehrmeyer, Karen Zeller; all artwork photographed by Tom Wacha

DANIELA BARNEA was born and raised in Jerusalem, Israel. She graduated with a BA in graphic design from the College of Arts and Crafts, Bezalel. She is currently enrolled at the California College of Arts and Crafts in Oakland and Foothill College in Mt.View, where she currently studies painting and printmaking.

PATI BRISTOW has explored as many media and methods as possible, combining them to create works of art. Her greatest joy is to work collaboratively with others, sharing time, space, and artistic passions. Please visit her website, pati-bristow.livejournal.com.

KYOKO FISCHER is a Bay Area printmaker and painter originally from Tokyo, Japan. She received her BFA from San Jose State, and she is currently working as a full-time painter. Her artwork can be viewed in various displays, from galleries to hotels, as well as on her own website, KyokoFischer.com.

INGE INFANTE studied art, photography, graphic design, and mathematics. This background, together with her love of music and travel, is reflected in her art in a fascinating combination of painting, drawing, printing, photography, computer graphics, and collage.

CAROL KEMP is a versatile artist living in the central coast of California. She is a mixed-media artist and presently working with metal. Carol and art partner Syd McCutcheon co-own the Art Clinic, a working studio in Solvang, California. Please visit her blog, faceaday.blogspot.com.

BIRTHE LINDHARDT lives in Denmark. She is an artist and a retired art teacher. She paints in acrylics and watercolor, collages, draws, and creates altered books and art journals. Please visit her website, lindhardt.org.

LAURA RYAN is a mixed-media artist who enjoys printmaking. She has shown her work in juried art shows, including the Riverside Art Museum, where she is a member. She is a member of two other art communities and enjoys sharing with other artists. Please visit her blog, eye-poppers.blogspot.com.

JULIE SNIDLE enjoys taking a variety of art classes across the United States. She has had work published in magazines and has donated art for charitable causes. Drawing, painting, encaustic, and collage are her focus right now.

LINDA STINCHFIELD is enjoying her retirement by learning new techniques and pursuing new skills. Her current enthusiasms are watercolor, alternative photographic processes, intaglio printmaking, and book arts.

ANNIE SWINCINSKI is a 2001 graduate of the Savannah College of Art and Design. She currently lives and works as a full-time artist out of her home studio in State College, Pennsylvania. Please visit her website, dwellinstyle.org.

MARISSA SWINGHAMMER is a fine-art printmaker living in Jamaica Plain, with her husband, baby girl, greyhound, and cat. Her prints are multi-layer, multi-block, one-of-a-kind woodcuts inspired by nature and her surroundings. Please visit her website, mleefineart.com.

RAE TRUJILLO received her BA from California State University, Hayward in 1978 with an emphasis in sculpture. She has always dabbled in a variety of art forms but fell in love with the book arts in 2004. Please visit her website, raesofsun.com.

ELIN WATERSTON is an award-winning textile/mixed-media artist and graphic designer. She is the Visual Arts Director, as well as an art instructor, at the Katonah Art Center in Katonah, New York, and is an Art*o*mat participating artist.

MIDGE WILLIAMS is a Seattle-area artist, specializing in monotypes and oil painting. She has a BFA in fine art from Western Washington University and has co-owned a printmaking lab in Seattle, teaching the solar-plate printmaking technique. She uses no press to create many of her prints and often uses mixed media in their production.